Read March 2014.

All rights of distribution, also by film, radio, television, photomechanical reproduction, sound carrier, electronic media and reprint in extracts, are reserved.

The author is responsible for the content and correction.

© 2014 united p. c. publisher

www.united-pc.eu

Looe Island then and now

By

Carolyn Clarke

Acknowledgements

In writing this book I relied heavily on the published works of Mike Dunn and David Clensey and thank them for allowing me to quote their works and for their helpful criticisms and suggestions. No work about Looe Island is complete without reference to Attie's two books, which have bought the Island alive for so many and without which, this work would not have been possible. My grateful thanks to Cornwall Wildlife Trust for giving permission to quote from these works and to all the current residents, Sheila and Gus, Mary and Patrick and Jon and, especially Claire who gave me invaluable help with regard to information on the role of the Island today. I would also like to thank Barbara Birchwood-Harper, for her help and advice on Looe Island Smugglers and to the staff of The Old Guildhall Museum in Looe who allowed me to look through their archive of newspaper cuttings and census returns regarding the Island.

For their invaluable comments on the manuscript, I would like to thank Ann Clayton, Betty Collings, Trish Durrant, Mo Fearnside; Robert Wilkins; Leena Batchelor; Sharon Copes and Fran Westrop. Thanks also to Chris Gray for his cartographical skills in drawing the map of Looe Island. Finally, heartfelt thanks to Patrick Gray, who shared my return, inspired me throughout the journey, and was unstinting in his help and advice throughout.

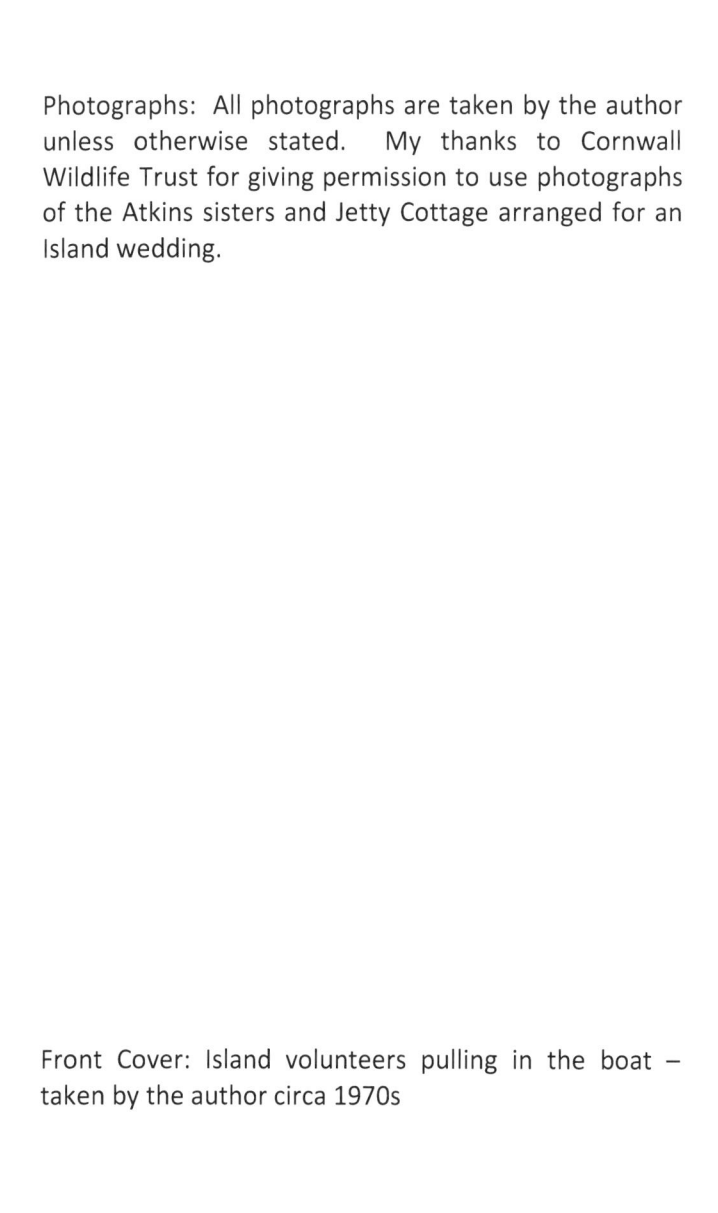

Photographs: All photographs are taken by the author unless otherwise stated. My thanks to Cornwall Wildlife Trust for giving permission to use photographs of the Atkins sisters and Jetty Cottage arranged for an Island wedding.

Front Cover: Island volunteers pulling in the boat – taken by the author circa 1970s

Looe Island

Looe Island Then and Now

To those who shared that special summer with me

Looe Island has fascinated visitors for many years and the adventures of the Atkins sisters have been, and remain, a popular collection of tales about island life.
Looe Island Then and Now adds a new perspective to this halcyon period, offering an insight to island life from the perspective of an enthusiastic volunteer.

In this enjoyable book it is clear how fondly Carolyn Clarke remembers her time on Looe Island. In recounting her experience of returning to the island the reader can share the deep impression left by the island and the Atkins sisters. After reading Looe Island Then and Now I hope it will inspire a visit to Looe Island. The reader can then discover the fascination of present day island life and how this wonderful place is now managed as a nature reserve by Cornwall Wildlife Trust.

Jon Ross
Warden for Looe Island Nature Reserve
Cornwall Wildlife Trust 2013

Chronology of Looe Island* Owners

Evidence of habitation on the Island as early as 800BC

Looe Island functioned as an early Christian settlement and centre of pilgrimage, which was purchased by the See of Glastonbury in 1144

1289 Glastonbury Abbey sold the property to a local landowner and the priory was replaced with a chapel served by a secular priest

1536 Following the Dissolution of the Monasteries, Looe Island became the property of the Crown and at some point afterwards the Island came into possession of the Mayow's of Bray

1600 John Trelawny purchased the Trelawne Estate from the Crown. John Trelawny was known as a staunch royalist during the English Civil War, whose family later purchased Looe Island.

1730 Burthogge Mayow sold Looe Island to Benjamin Salmon

1743 Looe Island purchased "for a trifling consideration" by Edward Trelawny Governor of Jamaica, MP for West Looe and owner of considerable amounts of land in Cornwall, including the Trelawne Estate. During this time the Island was leased to different tenants over that period, including the Finn and Hooper families

1921 The Trelawny family sold Looe Island and it was subsequently owned by different people who farmed the Island and fished the seas. By the 1940s daffodil farming was a major industry and this continued into the time that the last owners, Attie and Babs lived there.[i]

2004 Following the death of Babs Atkins the Island came into the ownership of Cornwall Wildlife Trust.

*Although referred to throughout as Looe Island. The Island has had a number of different names during its history and readers who would like to learn more details of these are referred to *The Looe Island Story:* Mike Dunn Pub. Polperro Heritage Press 2005 P.25-27

Introduction

To be detached from the problems of the world and live on your own private Island is a romantic idyll shared by many; if that island is only a short boat trip from the beautiful Cornish mainland and has its own buildings, electricity and water supply, the dream would surely dissolve into an economic fantasy. Nonetheless, two remarkable sisters, who had always cherished an ambition to own an island, made this vision a reality: they bought Looe Island.

In 1965 Evelyn Atkins (Attie) and her sister Roselyn (known as Babs, because she was the baby of the family) bought Looe Island, for just £22,000. The Island is the only Island in the British Isles known to have two official English names, as it is also known as St George's Island.[ii] Warmed by the Gulf Stream, Looe Island has been generous to its inhabitants, providing seaweed for fertilizer and a mild climate, which has enabled them to make extra money from crops of early vegetables and flowers. Yet, where nature gives, nature takes, and sometimes in winter Looe Island can be ravaged by storms and cut-off from the mainland for days on end. Waves have been known to lash against its shores destroying valuable possessions and even taking pieces of the very fabric of the Island in their wake, whilst icy winds will encircle the Island, lifting roof tiles and rattling windows.

Looe Island has an area of approximately 22.5 acres, and it remains today much as it was when Attie and Babs bought it, with three main buildings there; *Island House*, where the sisters lived; *Jetty Cottage*, which was built at the back of a stone-built rectangular barn, and was the place where Attie used to retreat to in later years in order to write her books[iii] , and *Smugglers' Cottage*. The barn and *Smugglers' Cottage* are the Island's oldest buildings, both are stone built and rectangular. *Smugglers' Cottage* backs onto the wooded area and faces out towards the Rame Peninsula and the sisters used it to provide accommodation for friends visiting the Island. On the death of Attie in 1997, Babs continued to live on the Island until she died on there in March 2004.

Following Attie's death, their friends Sheila and Gus Ravine moved into *Smugglers' Cottage* to help Babs with the day to day running of the Island. David Clensy, who had first visited Looe Island as a small boy with his parents, and then later as a volunteer in the 1990s, poignantly recalls in his book *Island Life*[iv]*,* how Sheila and Gus looked after Babs and nursed her, as she suffered and died from leukaemia. Today the couple still live on the Island, the tenancy of *Smugglers' Cottage* having been left to them by Babs for the rest of their lifetimes. Long before Attie's death the sisters talked about the Island's future. Originally, it was to be bequeathed to the National Trust but, following the National Trust's policy of selling off some of their properties, it was subsequently decided that Looe Island's future would be safest in the hands of Cornwall Wildlife Trust.

Situated just off the furthest tip of Looe Island lies Little Island, this tiny islet is a gull colony, which was separately bequeathed to the Trelawny family by the Atkins sisters. Little Island was subsequently re-named Trelawny Island and its reversion to the Trelawny family thus closes the circle of history; for this old

Cornish family owned Looe Island from 1743 until 1921. During that time the family built *Island House*[v] , which became Attie and Bab's home for nearly 40 years. In more recent times Sir John Barry, 13th Baronet Trelawny, has written a history of Looe Island [vi]and has also provided invaluable help to local historians, including the curator of *The Old Guildhall Museum* Looe, who drew on his extensive knowledge of Looe and its environs, when conducting her own research on Looe Island smugglers[vii]

Until recently[viii] *Island House* was left much as it was in Attie and Bab's time and visitors could sometimes visit it, accompanied by Sheila or Gus[ix] . At one time there was talk of turning it into a wildlife observatory and visitors centre; however, as Cornwall Wildlife Trust Warden, Claire, explained to me, a Trust does not have much flexibility with regard to changing the usage of a building. Fittingly, the lease of Island House has now been granted to Mary and Patrick who live there and were the first couple to have been married on the Island. Mary first visited the Island in 1979 when she was 7, and she and her family stayed in *Smugglers' Cottage* every year from then on, with Mary and her brothers' segueing into volunteering as they hit their teens.

The third couple that make up the Island community are the two wardens, Claire and Jon, who live in *Jetty Cottage*.   Weather permitting, the Island is open to the public for nine months of the year and in summer, the population of the Island is swelled by volunteers and visitors, which sometimes include wedding parties, and temporary residents who can experience living on the Island by hiring a tipi.

*

Attie and Babs were not fabulously wealthy individuals looking for an Island retreat; they had relatively modest financial means, and therefore the Island needed to be self-financing, whilst still remaining true to their vision of a largely non-commercial enterprise that would not impact on its natural beauty and history.

When the sisters bought the Island, electricity was produced by means of a rather temperamental oil-fired generator and fresh water was pumped from an underground spring. Although Attie and Babs grew their own fruit and vegetables, a lot of provisions still needed to be transported in from the mainland and rates and taxes were exorbitant. Economic survival dictated that Bab's teaching income was essential, and this necessitated her living on the mainland during weekdays and term times. On the other hand, someone needed to be there to look after the Island and almost from the day of purchase onwards; Attie lived on the Island full-time.

In order to boost the Island income, and provide hospitality for the increasing numbers of tourists and friends who wanted to visit the Island, Attie ran a tearoom. In addition, this indomitable lady continued the existing Island business of growing and selling early daffodils and potatoes for the London market. The sisters also had a pottery studio where they made beautiful ceramics, which they sold in their Craft Centre; they were keen on lapidary too and made jewellery and ornaments from polished stones and driftwood found on the Island.

The sisters' vision for the future of Looe Island was that it would always remain a self-sufficient little piece of paradise. Attie's memoirs[x] draw the reader in as she recounts through stories and reminiscences the ways in which their dreams for the Island are realised, with each tale evoking an image of a different life, different times and perhaps a different perspective.

One of the early projects for the Island was to advertise for student volunteers to live on the Island and, in return for helping to run the tearoom and maintaining the Island, they would be given a unique experience in a magical and special place. I was one of those volunteers and this is my story, yet in many respects the story of Looe Island belongs to everybody who has ever visited the Island and come under its spell. A summer vacation in the early 1970s enabled me to begin to understand the Atkins sisters and their vision for the Island, as I learnt of shipwrecks and buried treasure, smuggling and ghosts, wildlife and legends. I saw an abundance of wildlife, but also witnessed death and carnage, I heard of myth and magic and strange examples of synchronicity. Now more than 40 have years passed and the Island calls me back once more.

Chapter 1

Then and Now

The 1960s and 70s were another age, almost a 'foreign country', where young people tended to be more innocent and childhood could extend well into the late teens. It was a time that pre-dated the electronic, virtual world of today; an era when even photography required several reels of film and good light conditions; yet significantly, we were less hidebound by rules and bureaucracy and in this respect life was easier. Inflation and rampant speculation were still phenomena of the future, and in retrospect, an air of optimism and self-belief pervaded those carefree years and perhaps provided the backdrop for the Atkins sisters' dream.

Life is always a question of timing, and for several decades a return visit to Looe Island was not possible, as the demands family and career took priority. Additionally, the old adage of "don't look back, you may be disappointed", was lodged in my mind and a part of me wanted to treasure those summer days as a special and unique experience, rather than run the risk of having those memories altered in any way.

Nonetheless the desire to keep Looe Island encapsulated in the world of my imagination changed on a Friday morning in 2012 when, I noticed Mike Dunn's book *The Looe Island Story* [xi] on the shelves of my local library; I then re-read my old copies of Attie's memoirs. Within days of re-reading *We Bought an Island,* I turned on television to find that the Channel 4 Time Team 2008 excavation of Looe Island and Lamanna was being repeated. A few days later a friend invited me over for coffee and the oil painting in her front room was of Looe Harbour. I discovered that she was Cornish by birth and knew Looe well. Coincidences were beginning to pile up; a friend was working with his son on building a boat in Cornwall and suggested that we had a holiday to include a visit Looe Island.

Remembering all the fortuitous meetings and coincidences that enabled Attie and Babs to buy their Island, I realised that something was telling me that the moment had come to share and re-live those teenage memories.

Chapter 2

Thoughts and Impressions

In the words of L. P Hartley, "The past is a foreign country; they do things differently there"[xii] and so it was for me as I recall a summer in the early 1970s when my Mother drove me from my home town in the heart of the West Midlands to Birmingham's New Street Station and I caught "The Cornish Man" to "An Island somewhere off the coast of Looe".

I would have done things differently had I been older and wiser. I would have recorded all my memories, I would have taken numerous photographs, I would have stayed in touch with the four students that I shared my summer with and I would have listened far more carefully and intently to Attie and Babs' stories about their part in the Island's history. As things were, I only took four poor-quality, blurred photographs with my Brownie box camera and the wonderful cards and letters sent to me every Christmas by the sisters failed to survive house and life changes as my world moved on. I only briefly kept in touch with one of my fellow student workers, and even that reminder of former times was a contact that soon petered out, as marriage, jobs and babies took over our separate lives.

My memories of Looe Island are disparate and eclectic, some events are so clearly embedded in my brain that they seem to have happened yesterday; whilst equally there are huge gaps in my recall, as my mind has selected, re-organised, exaggerated and deleted. My history of two weeks working on a Cornish Island in the early 1970s is both shared and unique and interwoven with it will be the history of the Island itself comprising information, perceptions and images that I amassed during that summer together with facts gleaned from the research of others, most especially from Evelyn Atkins' two accounts of the sisters' Island life.

I am fortunate that a number of people have written about this magical island, enabling me to draw on factual information to prompt my recall and fill in the gaps in my own memories. The Island has a rich and engaging history, a largely undamaged ecology, smugglers, burials, hidden treasure and Biblical connections; some say that Jesus once walked on its shores; there are also numerous tales of the Island becoming meshed into the wider historical context of the times, from cannon balls reputedly fired from the Spanish Armada, being washed up onto its shores, to the rusting remains of a WWII aircraft and a Victorian boathouse surfacing with the driftwood. Most intriguing of all, is a crater from a WWII bombing lying half hidden in the Island woodland; apparently the Germans mistook Looe Island for an English battleship.

The sisters advertised the Island in the language and mores of the 1960s as:-

> Open to day visitors (landing fee payable) in the summer. This is a non-profit making venture, the landing fees and other income being devoted to conserving the island's natural beauty and to providing facilities for visitors without commercialising it in any way. There are no roads, no shops and no traffic. There is safe bathing, fishing, two beaches, a natural rock swimming pool, rocky coves, caves and woodland walks. Island crafts and copies of the two books are on sale for the Island

> Conservation Fund. In summer, volunteers undertake projects on the island. These are encouraged by the National Trust and the British Trust for Conservation Volunteers and have been featured in various radio and television programmes and in the regional and national Press. These voluntary working holidays are self-catering and are suitable for families, students and active OAPs. [xiii]

The information probably spoke as much about the sisters as it did about the Island and there are some obvious omissions. For example, there is no mention that the Island also contained the ruins of a Celtic chapel or had three dwelling places. *Island House,* where the sisters lived, was the largest of these buildings and its impressive gabled exterior belied the fact that downstairs there were only two sizeable rooms, the sitting room and the kitchen. *Island House* was built in 1876 by the Trelawny family, in order that the family had somewhere to live on the Island, for the fishing and hunting seasons. The sycamore woodland area of the Island was also planted around this time to help shelter crops and provide cover for shoots.

Smugglers' Cottage and the barn in front of *Jetty Cottage*, were much earlier buildings and more or less contemporary with one another having been constructed in the early eighteenth century; *Jetty Cottage* was, in effect a room which was added behind the old barn, which now served as the Island Tearoom/Craft Centre/Visitors' Centre.

When I was living on Looe Island, there was accommodation provided for up to six students, in three wooden huts which ran down in a line towards the jetty. The huts had no water or electricity, and the lack of heating rendered them unsuitable for occupation during the cold seasons. In those days there were no self-catering facilities for volunteers and so Attie cooked us meals, which we ate in the Craft Centre. Reading Attie's memoirs some years later, I realised for the first time what a chore and expense it must have been for her, nonetheless in looking after us so well, Attie 'created' many happy hard-working volunteers.

Attie and Babs were about the same age as my parents and perhaps we were as surrogate children to them, they certainly felt like mothers to me in the way they cared for and cosseted us and, on occasions, disciplined us, when we behaved like the 'typical teenagers' that we all were.

My story is of just a moment in the Island's history, it is of a time when things were done differently, a time of possibilities and adventures and of two sisters who had invited a group of young people into their home and lives to share their dreams.

Chapter 3

The Journey

Disparate memories flood back as I recall standing on a cold, windy, Birmingham railway platform clutching a couple of bags of clothes and possessions and waiting for *The Cornishman* to arrive. Attie's letter had instructed me not to "bring too much with you", before enumerating the items which would be useful, including a torch and sensible shoes.

I remember that I felt a mixture of apprehension and excitement as I boarded the train. In those days each railway carriage had a narrow corridor running the length of the train; with doors going off to the compartments where the passengers sat; each compartment housed twin seats which faced each other, there was lots of polished wood everywhere, and mirrors and railway posters on the wall. The seats were covered with an itchy carpet-like material and if you hit them clouds of dust flew out. I had the compartment all to myself for most of the journey – my own little world –.

Finally the train arrived at Liskeard, where I caught the local connection to Looe, noticing as I disembarked, that there was a model of a Cornish pixie on the headboard. Every summer *The Cornishman* conveyed hoards of holidaymakers from the Midlands to the Cornish Riviera. During this era, the trains were diesel powered, but still retained some of the glamour of the steam days with their corridors and individual compartments and polished mahogany woodwork;

although I don't think they all had pixies sitting on their engines.

As I settled myself into the dark wood compartment with the itchy seat, Attie's handwritten letter clutched in my hand, I speculated as to why I had been chosen to help on this Island. It was not as easy to research places in the 1970s as it is today, and I knew nothing about St George's Island when I applied to work there, equally Attie's letter failed to provide any clues. I wondered if the Island was a big concern, run something along the lines of Camp America. As would be expected, I mulled over how many people might have applied for the job and what qualities they were looking for in their volunteers.

The Island work was advertised on the Student Union Notice Board. In the era of the early 1970s, nobody worried about getting a job, it was simply a matter of which one you would choose, the same was also true of holiday work the world over. By the Spring Term, several sheets of closely typed A4 paper had gone up on the NUS notice board advertising holiday work. Many of the student jobs advertised were abroad; grape picking in France or working on a Kibbutz in Israel; the latter work especially appealed to me, but with the country still in the middle of the October War (1969-73) my parents were understandably nervous about me going out to the Middle East. Perhaps we stayed children longer at that time, certainly my life was more sheltered than it is for many teenagers today, I would not have thought to challenge my parents' decision and, swallowing my disappointment, I returned to the NUS notice board.

The advertisement for student volunteers on St George's Island was somewhere towards the bottom of the list, and although the work was not in some faraway country, it sounded exotic and different. I had never been to Cornwall but we had visited Devon on a number of family holidays and I imagined that a Cornish Island would not be too different from the sand, rocks, seagulls and rolling Atlantic waves of my 'Devon holidays'. In the world of the early 1970s there was nothing strange or remarkable at all about 6 teenagers living on an island in three wooden sheds with two middle aged ladies who had a dream.

The letter told me nothing beyond the dates that I would be staying and that I would not need much apart from sensible footwear and a torch. I was also told that I must take any rubbish I created home with me. Again, I mulled over the question of what made the sisters choose me from among the available applicants and how many students had applied for the work and how many other students would be working with me. It all felt so exciting; an explorer visiting uncharted territory.

I wonder now, what the two sisters must have thought each time new volunteers arrived. I had given them little information about myself beyond the fact that I was studying Business Management and 'always wanted to visit Cornwall and live on an Island'. There was no interview or request for references, and in hindsight the whole concept of a two women on their own with somewhat unreliable telecommunication links to the mainland giving their home over to unknown young people was a brave, and some may say, foolhardy thing to do.

As I soon discovered, Attie was different from anybody else I had ever met; she was perceptive and intuitive, she did not need CV's and references to assist in the decision making process. Above all else, Attie held an exceptionally strong belief in the power of the Island to attract and repel. On several occasions she talked to me about this magnetism, and also writes about it in her memoirs; only those that loved, respected and understood the Island would be drawn to its shores.

Nonetheless there were a few basic selection criteria. Most obviously was a 'first come first served' criterion and those volunteers who had worked on the Island before and proved their worth were always valued. More tellingly, an independent streak was important. Those volunteers who wrote asking if they and their friend could work on the Island had their requests politely declined. In hindsight I think that the sisters would have preferred a better ratio of boys to help with the heavy manual work, and clearly as my little group comprised three girls and two boys, a lot more girls than boys must have applied to work on the Island.

Attie had worked in Personnel Management in her earlier life and, I felt, had an intuitive understanding of team building and the best way of getting a job done. If, for example, 'best friends' were to arrive to work on the Island, the chances were that they would remain in little exclusive cliques and maybe lack the self-containment and independent mindset that Island living required. Additionally, as a self-contained and independent character herself, Attie would naturally be drawn to others who shared these qualities, as would Babs, who as a teacher, would have acquired strong perceptual skills and a good knowledge of how the minds of young people 'worked'.

*

Whilst I sat in my polished wood capsule, the countryside rolled past. In due course I caught the local train at Liskeard, and reached my destination in the late afternoon. I remember as the train approached Looe I could look out of the window and see what I thought to be the sea on one side of the train. Some forty years later I discovered that 'the sea' was in fact, Looe Estuary.

Looe station is situated in East Looe and on alighting from the train I walked towards the main town area by way of the harbour; all the time I was scanning the horizon for the Island and a mild panic began to set in as I walked on, having failed in my quest to find Looe Island. Calming myself, I walked into a little café where I hoped that somebody could direct me; it smelt of salt and seaweed and fish, over-laid with strong tea and frying. Condensation was streaming down the windows, tea was being served from a large urn on the counter, the chairs were painted white and had vinyl seats, the tables were topped with pale yellow Formica, and the floor had rubber tiles; indeed everything about the café was practical and serviceable.

The cafe was crowded and muggy, and I was the only female customer there. By luck and chance, I had found the locals café. All the men at the little tables were fishermen, who had just come in after the afternoon's catch. Fortunately, they must have seen how confused and bewildered I looked, and took pity on me. When I asked how to get to Looe Island one of the men immediately offered to take me over in his boat. He introduced himself as Wren Toms and I later learnt that he was a great friend of Attie and Babs.

Alongside memories of the magic of the Island itself, is the memory of the kindness and hospitality of the fishing community of Looe. I subsequently learnt that, aside from the kindness shown to me, they all kept a watchful 'fatherly eye' on Attie. Although I did not know it then, Attie sometimes spent weeks alone on the Island in winter time; but nonetheless the boat owners and fishermen of Looe would bravely venture out whenever possible to ensure that she was not running short of supplies and (especially) that the Island generator had enough fuel.

As it was the first week of the school holidays, Babs would be staying on the Island throughout our stay; she was expected on the Island later on that evening, when she had finished her work at school.

As the boat neared the shore three figures ran towards it; two young men and a girl with long red hair and floral skirt. The fisherman threw them a rope and they hauled us to shore. After I had disembarked, the three volunteers pushed the boat back into sea and introduced themselves as Phil, Mike and Val. Phil asked me to follow them up a fairly steep shingle path to meet Attie.

Looking back it did seem to be a strange coincidence that on arrival at Looe Harbour I had just happened to find someone to row me over to the Island, and that the three Island volunteers had spotted the boat and been ready to greet me. Of course, the reality was that Attie would have alerted her fishermen friends in Looe to look out for me; she always knew when boats were expected to arrive at the Island and there was a telescope fixed at a high point near the house where you could watch for boats leaving the mainland. In those days, since there was no mobile landing jetty, the boats needed to be dragged on to the sand, and then pushed out to sea again on departure. This was one of our duties as volunteer helpers.

The Arrival

Chapter 4

Introductions were made and then the three volunteers led me to a stone-built rectangular building, which was originally the old barn at the front of *Jetty Cottage*, and now served as the Island Tearoom and the place where the Island crafts were displayed and sold. This building also doubled up as 'our space' in the evenings and was the room where we would congregate and take our meals together. The building had been known variously as the Transit Camp and the Visitor Centre and at one point in its existence it had also served as a venue for musical evenings and concerts on the Island. Unsurprisingly it was then known as The Music Room.

Attie and Babs were always kind and hospitable. On several occasions during my stay we had been invited into the large, welcoming kitchen of *Island House* to share food and drinks with them, nonetheless, the sisters were sensible enough to know that they would also need their own time and space when the day visitors had left, and so would we. Therefore the tearoom provided the perfect place for us when the day's work was done.

After a cup of tea and a lovely warm homemade scone, Attie showed me to my sleeping quarters, where I could leave my bags and settle myself before her sister Babs arrived from the mainland. Babs was a great support for Attie, the sisters were very close and she would bring a large proportion of the week's provisions over with her on a Friday night

In retrospect, there was so much about my time on the Island that I had taken for granted. For example, apart from some home grown vegetables and soft fruits in summer, there was no food on the Island and water was a precious commodity. Basics such as fuel, books, and writing materials had to be brought in, and rubbish had to be shipped back to the mainland. Yet in those far off days, the appearance of food at the table and lights in the house were just accepted without any consideration on my part as to how they got there, and it is a testament to the sisters' formidable organizational skills that I barely noticed the logistics of Island survival, away from the facilities of the mainland.

Looe Island is roughly the shape of a turtle, the 'hump of the turtle's shell' created a rise to the summit of the Island where there are stones marking the site of an ancient chapel. The huts where we slept formed a little cluster of buildings with *Island House* and the Tearoom and *Jetty Cottage*, whilst *Smugglers' Cottage* was further down and overlooked a sandy spit of beach. From the back it was hidden by woodland. *Smugglers' Cottage* and the landing beach below face the sparsely populated Rame Peninsula. Unlike the other buildings on the Island, *Smugglers' Cottage* cannot be seen when approached by boat from the mainland, and, as such, would have made a perfect place for receiving smuggled goods.

My sleeping quarters comprised a wooden garden shed, with a window on one side and bunk beds alongside the other; there was also a little table and chair and rug alongside the window. Tomorrow, another girl would be joining me. Altogether there were three volunteer sheds forming a line; Phil and Mike shared the end one and Val had the middle one and my shed was the one furthest away from *Jetty Cottage,* looking directly out to the sea, a pathway lead up from the huts to the Tearoom and *Island House.*

The following morning I learnt from Attie that another girl was supposed to have been joining Val yesterday, but had failed to turn up. It was not the first time that Attie had experienced volunteers failing to turn up, and doubtlessly it would not be the last. Nonetheless Attie's attitude towards such slights and discourtesies was always very philosophical, as she believed that the mystical self-selection mechanism of the Island was at work, ensuring that only those who would fit into Island life would choose to be there.

A lavatory block served the tearoom and doubled up as our facilities at night. In those balmy summer nights a walk along a little gravel path, lit by a thousand stars, was no real hardship, and one abiding memory of that summer on the Island was when Meg (who joined me the following evening) and I walked to the block, prior to settling down for a night's sleep. The sky was dark turquoise, the first stars were beginning to shine and the air was full of and hundreds of little 'birds' that seemed to be fluttering about our heads.

Being a town dweller, I did not realize at the time that the tiny flying creatures were bats; however as a country girl, Meg knew such things and quickly enlightened me. In hindsight, the Island played a very important role in my adolescent years in numerous ways; I learnt so much in such a short time, and the Island's wildness and beauty stimulated a life-long love of the natural world.

*

As I put my bags at the bottom of the bunk and sat on the chair I mulled over my first impressions. The shed was warm and smelt of cedar, it was completely perfect for my needs. Although there was no artificial lighting, the window let in plenty of sunshine in the daytime; a chair to sit on, an area to put my bags down, and a table to rest a book or two on was all that I needed.

Meg arrived the next day and, despite the lack of space, we quickly developed accommodation routines, such as taking it in turns to get up first. The sheds were, in any case purely dormitories, and the Island provided us with all the space and privacy that we could ever dream of during those relatively few times when we were not working or in each other's company.

A decade or more later after Attie had published her two memoirs[xiv] , I discovered that by the late 1970s, in order to relieve herself of the task of cooking for volunteers, all of whom seemed to consume inordinate amounts of food, Attie had decided to provide self-catering facilities for them. Electricity was added to the volunteer accommodation, which was a large white hut with cooking facilities, below Island House and near where our huts would have stood. This volunteer hut was described by Attie as 'The Chalet'.

Attie memoirs[xv] recall that, this proved to be a wrong and very costly decision. The Island generator only switched itself off at night if all the switches were turned off; inevitably some volunteers forgot to turn off all the power when they went to bed and the generator would continue to operate throughout the night, landing the sisters with huge fuel bills[xvi]

Volunteers' Chalet. (Carolyn Clarke June 2013)

This was a later addition, which provided Island volunteers with self-catering facilities

Chapter 5

Attie and Babs

Soon after I had alighted on the Island, Babs also arrived. It was the first day of the school holidays and Attie must have been anticipating this welcome moment for a long time. Whilst the sisters spent time catching up with each other in *Island House,* the four of us ate supper in the Tearoom and exchanged information about one another. Later that evening, Attie and Babs invited us to join them at *Island House* for a bedtime drink – not just a cup of tea - (although we had that too) but a glass of sweet, elderflower champagne, that tasted of honey and hedgerows and summer. Even now, I only have to think of *Island House* Champagne and I can feel the bubbles exploding on the back of my throat and the commensurate lightening of my head, which gave the whole evening something of a surreal feeling.

I later discovered that wine making was one of Attie's many talents and that she had brought all of her stocks of wine and champagne over with her. As can be imagined, the safe dispatch of large barrels of wine to the Island proved to be something of a challenge, described in some detail in Attie's memoirs. In retrospect I cannot help thinking that it was a pity that none of the smugglers who used to inhabit the Island were still living there, for doubtlessly they would have known exactly how to get barrels of alcohol ashore!

*

When I had stepped off the boat and onto the shores of Looe Island, I had focused on weighing up the other volunteers, considering how we would all get on together, and what work I would be required to do. Later on, when I was safe and secure in the warmth of *Island House's* stone-flagged kitchen, I began to observe the two sisters more closely.

Initial impressions of Attie and Babs were that they were quite difficult to tell apart, as facially they looked similar to one another and appeared at first sight, to be dressed almost identically. Both sisters had rosy apple cheeks and round glasses; a full time professional career on the mainland, was reflected in Bab's slightly neater appearance and more coiffured hair, whereas Attie had all the appearance of one who had been exposed to the Island elements and, through necessity, sorted out the temperamental generator and worked the land.

Babs and Attie must have had an exceptionally close relationship, for whilst I know of many people who enjoy their sibling's company, being confined on an island together and sharing in its trials and tribulations, would surely have presented its challenges. Later I learnt from Attie's memoirs that they did have their arguments, but only over trivial issues, being totally united in all the important decisions made. To me, the two sisters appeared to operate as a well-oiled machine, where the moving parts were completely in tune with one another.

Mentally, I labelled Attie as the more outgoing sister, tough, capable and practical, Babs seemed quieter and less out-spoken. Attie had attended pottery classes as well as being a professional photographer who did her own developing; she had lapidary skills and had in the past run wine making courses. Babs too was a skilled craftsman and later on, during a rainy morning spent in their pottery studio, she showed us how to make simple pendants which would be fired and glazed for sale in the craft shop. It was only at that point during my stay that I felt I had got to know her as well as I had Attie, for during my first evening she was the quiet observer who allowed Attie to apprise us about the Island and our role there.

Attie's book *We Bought an Island*[xvii] describes how Babs had bought and developed a school before her present job teaching in Looe; she certainly was an inspirational teacher, patient, kind and encouraging, when one cold and miserable morning she allowed us all to have a go at making Island crafts. Looking back on my time on Looe Island, I have often wondered what happened to the pottery studio and all the work created there.

Island House looked out onto a lawn with flower beds and its garden formed one of the really vivid visual memories I have of life on the Island. The garden was always full of butterflies and bees which loved the nectar-rich hebes planted there; and roses dropped carpets of petals on the lawn. At night time lilies scented the night air attracting velvet moths.

Long before it was fashionable, the sisters had a strong commitment to organic gardening and environmental issues. There must have been a lot of aphids around that year, as on one occasion I remember discussing 'the greenfly problem' with Attie. I mentioned that my grandfather used a spray of green soft soap mixed with water (which I think was a type of shampoo still available in the 1970s) to cure the aphid problem. Both sisters seemed very interested in this remedy and were going to investigate its ecological credentials further, with a view to buying green soft soap from the chemist's shop at Looe.

Reflecting on the Island house and the evening in the kitchen drinking the elderflower champagne, I recall that the room was in many ways as one would think of a farmhouse kitchen. There were grey flagstones on the floor, large oak beams and a scrubbed pine table. An Aga with two chairs either side of it provided a focal point. There was probably a rug by the fire and I seem to recall the sisters' black and white Border collie, Kim sleeping on it. I think that we probably sat at the table and Attie and Babs in the fireside chairs.

Whilst my memory of the kitchen is fairly hazy, I can still recall some objects in lucid detail; perhaps memory is like this, we alight on a few specific details of time and place whilst the bigger picture fades away. The minutiae of detail etched on my brain included an old dresser and shelves, which were full of books on natural history and Cornish history alongside classic novels and some 'pulp literature'; for everything about the sisters was eclectic, from their taste in books to their museum of curiosities on the mantel shelf and dresser, which included an ivory-coloured bone of some sea creature, a piece of driftwood with a speckled wood butterfly painted on it and various china ornaments. I wondered if a close family member had painted the butterfly, if Attie was here today I'd ask her. I also wished that there were some painted butterflies for sale in the craft shop, as I'd have loved to have taken one home with me.

On the mantel piece a 1930s wooden clock was ticking with a beat that seemed to keep time with the swish of the tides, and along the open shelves were demi-johns of wine, their colours ranging from the delicate straw of the elderflower champagne through to rich ambers, gold and ruby reds winking and refracting the light with their jeweled brilliance. The tick of the clock, the glow of the elderflower champagne, the sleeping cats and the welcome of the old kitchen remain as vivid as yesterday and finally as the turquoise sky turned to black and stars began to appear, we all made our way to our huts and I settled into bed.

As I lay in my bunk bed I could touch the wooden walls and see pictures in the chipboard patterning of the roof, the cedar wood still smelt tangy and exotic whilst through the window a crescent moon was shining. It seemed completely silent but my ears soon became attuned to a soft swishing sound, as the sea lapped the shore and lulled me to sleep.

Attie (left) and Babs enjoying a glass of their home made elderflower champagne in Jetty Cottage circa 1970 Courtesy Cornwall Wildlife Trust

Chapter 6

The Tearoom

The dawn was all movement and light, as I woken by gold, green, red and electric blue colours sparkling through the flimsy curtains and gaps in the timbers of my hut. The strength of the sun caused the cedar wood walls to cast a red-gold glow over the room and in the corner of the window a damp cobweb sparkled with prismatic lights. There was heavy dew outside and once again the sea was quietly washing the shore. In the far distance I could hear seagulls screeching to each other with delight at the new day, and these sounds reminded me that I was lying in a little hut perched on a Cornish Island.

Remembering where I was, but completely forgetting any information I might have been given, I dressed and made my way to the Craft Centre. Val, Phil and Mike were already there eating breakfast at one of the tables. As they had all been on the Island for a few days, they knew the routine; the boys mended fences, cleared paths and helped with general maintenance work. Phil was also engaged in digging a reservoir in the woodland area; their first job of the day was to collect sea water to fill the water storage tank that serviced the Island's lavatories.

Whilst the boys fetched the water and commenced their maintenance tasks, Val and I, armed with a brush and duster, began our days' work in the Craft Centre. Val explained that the tearoom had to be ready to receive visitors by 10.00 when the first boat would be arriving. Prior to the arrival of visitors, we had to dust the display shelves and sweep the floor; wipe down and set the tables and make sure that the fridge contained enough provisions to make sandwiches and snacks; when this work was completed, our next duty was to go over to *Island House* to help Attie with the baking of scones for the Cornish Teas.

Dusting the 'Island Crafts' for sale in the tearoom, I was mesmerized by the polished stones which had been made into different pieces of jewelry and ornaments. During last night's conversation, Attie had told us that semi-precious stones could be found on the Island shores; these included rose quartz, amethyst, carnelians, banded agate and moss agate. All these polished specimens were for sale in the Island Craft Centre, each beautifully turned and smooth as glass.

My eye was drawn to a large moss agate mounted on a flat, slate-coloured stone. The agate was an intense dark bluish-black, with a tracery of white quartz in it, looking like ice flowers against a dark sky. I wanted to buy that particular stone so much, but being big and beautiful, it was priced beyond my holiday budget. Nonetheless, I used to look at this stone every day whilst dusting the display shelves and it was always a relief to me that none of the Island visitors bought it, causing me to have to witness it leaving the Island and its place on the Craft Centre shelves. I wonder now what happened to that moss agate stone and all the other Island crafts; I hope that they are all loved and sitting in thousands of different homes across the world reminding the owners of time spent in a very special place.

In her book [xviii]*We Bought an Island,* Attie describes their interest in gemology and recalled the many absorbing hours that she and Babs spent collecting gemstones in the West Country. Another theme in her memoirs was that of the phenomena of synchronicity. For example, Attie appeared to always meet the people she needed to meet at exactly the right moment and, whilst skeptics may attribute the many chance encounters recounted in her memoirs as mere coincidence, both sisters did seem to possess an uncanny power to draw people to them and make the seemingly impossible happen. Additionally, on several occasions, Attie spoke of her belief in providence and magic. A story in *We Bought an Island* which perfectly illustrated this belief happened in the courtyard of their cottage on mainland Looe. During the process of sorting and examining their gemstone finds, Attie was mentally mulling over the possibility of buying Looe Island and wishing that they could find a way of being able to afford it. Very soon afterwards the way was indeed shown to her, and thereafter Attie remained firmly convinced that one of the gemstones that she had touched had worked some magic for them.

Re-reading *We Bought an Island* nearly forty years later, I realized then how similar a lot of my own interests were to Attie and Babs', for I spent many a happy childhood hour scouring the Wren's Nest Hills, looking for the rare trilobite *Calymene blumenbachii,* which always eluded me. Nevertheless, I invariably bought back a bag of interesting pebbles and sometimes beautiful shell and coral fossils. Again, in common with Attie and Babs, I could never go to a beach without having to forage for pretty shells and interesting pebbles and driftwood. Needless to say, I was really excited at the thought of being able to find semi-precious gemstones on the Island beach to bring back to the Studio for tumbling and polishing.

Sadly, my gemology ability did not match up to Attie's and I failed to find even one really special stone during my stay on the Island, although I did notice a number of pure white egg-shaped and round pebbles, that I believe are prized by ancient peoples as having magical properties. In hindsight I have reached the conclusion that my lack of success in finding semi-precious stones on the beach was not because they were not there, but because I lacked the practiced 'eye' and patience and skill of the gemologist. Any visitor who bought one of the polished stones from the Craft Centre would not only be buying both a product of the Island but also a special treasure lovingly identified and worked by Attie or Babs.

With the cleaning finished, Val and I made our way over to *Island House*. Attie used to buy dry scone mix in huge sacks from the mainland and by the time we had swept and dusted and laid the tables, she had mixed up the first batch of scones in her Kenwood food mixer and put them in the Aga. On arrival in the kitchen, we were given aprons and bowls of the wet dough to form into scones and bake, ensuring that they were all near enough the same size. When baked, we carefully carried the scones over to the tearoom kitchen. The cream and butter were already in the fridge and we spent the next few minutes spooning jam into dainty little pots and cutting pats of butter. Val suggested that I prepare some grated cheese ready for the sandwiches. The grater was a traditional metal sort and the job took longer than I expected. Later, I horrified Attie by suggesting that it would be quicker to just slice up some pieces of cheese. She patiently cut two equal chunks of cheese and grated one piece, whilst cutting the other into thin slices before asking me how many sandwiches I expected to make with the cut slices. It was self-evident; grated cheese went a lot further than sliced cheese, and so that morning I learnt an important culinary lesson - if you want to make food go further, grate it first -. Fortunately for my tired wrists, the other ingredients of tomatoes, cucumber and ham did not lend themselves to such treatment and only needed slicing in readiness for the Island visitors.

In another age, we might have had to undertake 'food hygiene' training. The scones would no doubt have had to be weighed to ensure uniformity and Attie and Babs would probably have hovered round to make sure we were doing everything correctly. However in those bygone days we were simply trusted to just get on with things and feed the hungry visitors.

The boys meanwhile were looking out through the old Island telescope, situated at a high spot on the Island near the main house, for the boat bringing visitors to the Island. As soon as this had been spotted, we would all run down the main shingle path to help drag the boat on to the shore. Once the boat had been pulled to shore, one of us would run up to *Island House,* here Attie and Babs would meet and greet the visitors outside the house and tell them something of the history of the Island, whilst advising on the best things to see and places to walk.

Ever thoughtful, Attie and Babs realised that when people visited the Island they would invariably want a drink and a bite to eat at some point during their stay.

Indeed some visitors were so charmed by the Island tearoom in *Jetty Cottage* that they never moved beyond its cosy confines, preferring to stay and enjoy hearing the sound of the sea from its warm interior, rather than to venture out and explore the Island. In many respects the tearoom was the beating heart of the Island and it came as no surprise to me to discover in later years that it was the place where Attie would write her books and Babs chose to spend her last days[xix]

It was a beautiful morning and the *Islander* brought a steady stream of visitors throughout the day. Val and I were kept constantly busy, especially as a number of visitors wanted to buy Island crafts. These days, the crafts would probably have been augmented with bought-in goods, such as, National Trust soap, beeswax furniture polish and Cornish Jams, but in the sisters time, visitors really did buy a genuine bit of Island history and the only items for sale not made on the Island itself, were the Arthur Dixon postcards, which I believe might have been produced from photographs taken by Attie[xx].

Whilst waiting for the arrival of the first Island visitors of the day, I was intrigued by three large pieces of worked stone standing near Island House; two were hexagonally shaped and all three were solid and heavy. I asked Attie if they had come as part of the effects of the Island, when they had bought Looe Island. Attie then explained that the stones had been found washed up on Jetty Beach and were rumoured to have been from the font belonging to the Island's ruined chapel.

Attie was a firm believer that the Island gave gifts to her and Babs from time to time. These particular stones had been washed ashore by the sea shortly after the sisters' arrival on the Island and therefore the timing was surely a sign of the Island's blessing on their custodianship. In *Tales from a Cornish Island*, published more than 10 years after my stay, I was fascinated to read about all the various gifts that the Island and its seas had given the sisters, for example, a china barn owl that can be seen photographed on the mantle-piece[xxi] amongst their eclectic and fascinating collection of ornaments. David Clensy recounts in his history of Looe Island[xxii] that the Owl was made of Beswick china and that it floated on the waves because it was stuffed with polythene. In Ancient Greece the goddess Athena, who represented wisdom and knowledge, was thought to disguise herself as an owl and to sight an owl was therefore very auspicious. Attie's owl was clearly a sign of favour from the Island, but sadly I have no memory of it during my stay and can only assume that it materialised at a later date.

I have always been fascinated by history, and when Attie mentioned the ruined chapel on the Island I wanted to know more; but as she wisely reminded me, the Island visitors would shortly be arriving and she had much to do first. We agreed to talk about the chapel in the evening when Babs and the other student helpers, were all together. Attie also mentioned that the new girl, Meg, would be arriving later on today and that maybe I should stop thinking about the chapel and instead focus on welcoming Meg, who would be sharing my sleeping quarters with me.

I had to admit that I had mixed feelings about being joined by another volunteer; already I had formed a bond with Val and three girls might be a crowd. I enjoyed having a room to myself; what if I did not 'gel' with the new girl? Not that there was any reason for thinking I should not; after all, the other three students were fantastic and I was looking forward to getting to know them better. With these thoughts whirring round, I saw Val running down from the shingle path to beckon me into the tearoom to help with service. In the distance, I could hear Phil talking to the first consignment of Island visitors on their way up the path to Island House. It was time to put the kettle on.

In its time Tearoom/Craft Centre had had several reincarnations, and immediately prior to becoming the Island Tearoom it had been used as a 'transit camp'[xxiii], where the sisters' possessions were stored, before more permanent resting places for them were found. It must have been an arduous task to sort and move everything, but the effort was well worthwhile, for the old barn was a lovely building with its own special atmosphere and a feeling of timelessness.

The long rectangular structure of the tearoom reflected its previous use as a barn. At one end there was a counter with cooking and washing up facilities behind it, whilst beyond that there were was the seating area with the crafts being displayed at the far end. Everything about the tearoom area was very olde worlde. The sisters loved antiques and crafts and when things broke, or were washed up on the shores they would mend and reuse, or find alternative lives for the recovered object. The tables and chairs in the tearoom may not have all matched each other, yet they blended in perfectly, some were antiques and others skilfully restored 'finds' , but all were dark, polished wood and gleamed in the light.

One of my favourite jobs was cleaning and polishing the tearoom, although realistically it was not a particularly high priority use of my time, considering all the more pressing things to be done on the Island. I seem to remember that each table was spread with a pretty table cloth, the cupboards in the kitchen area contained china and cutlery and many different sized china 'Brown Betty' teapots, the size being selected on the basis of whether a pot for one, two three or four people.

One side of the tearoom had windows looking out onto the lawn and across to the sea, whilst the other side sold Island crafts and a few postcards (which we all eagerly bought to write to friends and family). As mentioned earlier, there was never anything 'tacky' about the Island, no gift wrapped 'presents from Looe Island' made in London, or possibly Hong Kong.

In retrospect I can really appreciate the frustration that comes through in Attie's memoirs, for the whole process of survival and maintaining the Island would leave precious little time for her to spend on her craftwork. After all, one of the reasons that she and Babs had bought the Island was so that they could have time alone doing the things that they loved best. Further on into my stay on the Island, I have recounted the story of a morning spent with Babs in the pottery studio; time seemed to fly past and even now I can recall the complete contentment and feeling of well-being engendered by forming wet clay into different shaped pendants for sale in the shop. Although lured by the thought of lunch, it was still a real penance to leave the ceramics studio.

Serving in the teashop was demanding, fulfilling and great fun. The visitors always liked to have a chat and we never experienced any unpleasant or dissatisfied customers. Everybody seemed to be in 'holiday mode' and, of course, visitors were largely holiday makers, but maybe the atmosphere of self-containment and adventure that stepping on to an island evokes, together with the special magic and atmosphere of Looe Island, equally played a part. For I know from my experience of other jobs working in cafes and restaurants that pleasant and co-operative customers are not a fact of life that can invariably be guaranteed in all beautiful holiday resorts. Interestingly, many teashop customers so admired the work that Attie and Babs were doing and loved the Island so much that they would insist on paying over and above the asking price for their drinks. It was also noticeable that a number of visitors had been holidaying in Looe for many summers and an Island visit was an integral part of their holiday.

The other student helper, Meg, arrived with the final consignment of Island visitors. Whilst Val and I were busy in the tearoom, Attie and Babs had greeted her and gave her time to settle in. My first sight of Meg was sitting down in the outside eating area, looking at a book. She was a tall girl, with straight dark hair and a colouring that hinted at the enjoyment of an outdoor life, she was wearing light coloured shorts and a tee-shirt. Whilst Val and I were both town dwellers - Val from Walthamstow and I from the West Midlands - Meg was a country girl; she rode, and looked after animals on her parents' farm. Somewhere in the back of my mind I have the idea that she was going to study Equine Science but I might have been mistaken in this.

Memory does not treat all subjects equally and often erases the very details that you would like to recall; similarly I cannot remember what Val was going to be studying, possibly teaching or art, or maybe teaching art.

Meg was the most outgoing and least introspective of the three of us girls, she had a down-to-earth, practical approach to life, and appeared to a town-dweller like me, to have an encyclopaedic knowledge of country matters. Meg instantly had a rapport with the Island dog Kim, whereas I have always found the independence of cats a lot more engaging than the natural 'in your face' friendliness of most dogs. Needless to say, I never lost an opportunity to 'pet' the Island cats, Hamram and Joan[xxiv], who were named after two of the Smugglers from the Island's past.

Of the two male volunteers, Mike was the one that I knew the least about, but in common with all the volunteers, he was easy to get on with, pleasant and good company. Younger and more reticent than Phil, Mike's natural shyness, made him gravitate towards him, making the two of them almost inseparable. Phil was around the same age as we were, but appeared older because of his height and a charisma that seemed to imbibe him with a quiet confidence and authority. Having stayed on the Island for a number of summers, Phil knew a lot more about its workings than we did and we all at first, assumed that he was related to Attie and Babs in some way, as he definitely was a favourite with them.

Reading Attie's *Tales from our Cornish Island* [xxv]some years later I discovered that this Devonshire lad loved working on the Island so much that in total he stayed there for five consecutive summers, before finally pursuing a trainee managerial career with W.H Smith's. Every morning Phil (often accompanied by Mike) would disappear all day and we believed that he was doing heavy maintenance work, such as path clearing and fence mending/constructing, whilst we did the more 'feminine tasks', such as serving in the tearoom. There was also talk of Phil digging a reservoir somewhere in the woods, in order that winter rain could be stored to back up the existing water reserves, which were pumped from an underground well. Whilst the need for extra water in the summer was ever pressing and we were cautioned to exercise extreme economy with this precious commodity, it was only when reading Attie's *Tales*[xxvi] that I realised that the situation was not quite as it initially appeared, and despite the obvious need for a reservoir on the Island, this was not after all the real object of the exercise or the digging.

Attie the Author, answering questions about Island Life in winter to visitors in the Tearoom. The photograph was included in an article in *Woman's Own* following the publication of Attie's first book. *We Bought An Island* (Alan Meek/ *Woman's Own*) Photograph courtesy Cornwall Wildlife Trust

Chapter 7

Buried Treasure

The hidden network of caves on the Island, where ancient bones were said to protrude from the rocks, would have doubtlessly attracted tales of buried treasure. Arguably, if smuggled goods could be secreted on the island, then so too might treasure.

There have been many local stories of hidden caches of treasure on Looe Island and even rumours of a tunnel under the sea linking the Island to the mainland at Hannafore [xxvii]. Attie recalled that one day an ancient, and apparently authentic, treasure map arrived in the post. It had been sent by a clergyman from Cumbria who had previously visited the Island. The map showed the Island's earlier name of St Michael's Island[xxviii] and the clergyman claimed that the map had been in his family for generations. Attie went on to explain that everything about the map indicated that it was old and authentic[xxix]. This faded yellowing map indicated that treasure was buried on the Island at a spot somewhere in the woodland.

During the Nineteenth Century, rumours about the Island's treasure suggested that the location of any hidden hoard would be in a tunnel connecting the Island to the mainland, with the exit hole under the wooded area of the Island.[xxx] Attie records that she and Babs had agreed that the existence of the map would remain a secret. Five years later a descendent of the famous Island smuggler Amram Hooper visited the Island and confirmed the existence of the tunnel and showed the sisters the entrance, which had subsequently been blocked up with concrete.

Little did we know it then, but when Phil (and possibly Mike, although this is not recorded in Attie's book) disappeared to do maintenance work on the Island, including digging a second fresh water reservoir in the woodlands, they (or at least Phil) were also busily engaged in digging for this treasure.

Attie had instructed Phil as to the most propitious spot to dig, the spot being based on a combination of the treasure map and the results of dowsing. Unfortunately, despite spending five summers digging around this area, Phil never did find the treasure and both sisters decided to leave the possibility of its existence as a romantic dream, rather than continue with this somewhat fruitless endeavor.

The reservoir scheme was also abortive; although Phil had dug a huge and impressive 20 foot square hole going down well over 6 feet, the sisters discovered that there was a lot more to the science of reservoir building than simply digging a large water storage hole and lining it with cement. For example, a lid would also need to have been made to keep the water free from contamination. In the end it was realized that the cost and logistics were both prohibitive.

Using supplementary measures, such as conservation and re-use of water, the collection of rainwater in water butts and the use of sea water for non-drinking purposes, the sisters did manage all year round without the need for an additional fresh water supply.

Nonetheless, it must have been a constant worry for them.

Not many years after my stay on the Island, mainland Britain experienced the long hot summer of 1975 followed by the drought of 1976 and I reflected that during the period, when people on the mainland were fussing about their gardens drying up and hose pipe bans, Attie and Babs' worry must have been so much greater, with no rain to replenish their empty water butts.

Phil was a lovely person and a real workhorse. In retrospect, I cannot help wondering how much better employed he would have been helping and inspiring us all in our sessions in digging the vegetable plots in preparation for the winter crops, rather than 'searching for Smugglers' gold'. As for Mike, the one fact that really stands out in my mind about him, apart from being almost a smaller, quieter version of Phil, was that he had a passion for CB radio. Although Attie and Babs had radio phones and a highly effective signaling system when Babs was on the mainland, communication by CB radio must have seemed a very attractive proposition. I remember that the boys' hut looked like a ship in sail with a variety of masts and pieces of aerial sticking out over the roof and walls. To date I have not found any information as to whether, or not, this experiment was successful, but Mike was an electronics expert and, I think, Phil a keen and enthusiastic pupil. The two boys must have been most useful in helping Attie and Babs with the various temperamental gadgets on the Island and loved 'playing' with the generator, tractors and water pump.

In *Tales* Attie discussed the expense of thoughtless student volunteers forgetting to turn off lights at night because any light or electrical gadget left switched on would cause the generator to run throughout the night gobbling up precious fuel. Because Phil and Mike perfectly understood this concept, not only were they diligent about switching off lights at night themselves, but explained to us the importance of checking all the switches in the tearoom before turning in for the night; therefore I can categorically say that, thanks to Phil, none of us were guilty of causing the generator to fire up unnecessarily.

Our own accommodation huts did not have any power, and we had all arrived equipped with torches for bedtime reading; nonetheless, the sisters were still dependent on Island guests and volunteers remembering to turn off all the lights on the Island, as the generator would rather cleverly kick into life if any switch on the Island was turned on. I have since wondered why there was not a main switch in *Island House* that could be used to turn off all the lighting at a given time, and whether the generator was still capable of providing electricity for non-lighting purposes, such as the running of fridges, throughout the night. Clearly there must have been such a mechanism, but the logistics of its operation is unclear in Attie's account.

With introductions completed there was still work to be done in the tearoom. Later on, Attie and Babs had been invited to supper with the people staying in *Smugglers' Cottage*, so after bringing us a salad supper, they left us to spend the evening together. The following day was a Monday, which was generally a much quieter day, work-wise than Sunday; so before leaving us setting up the tearoom for the next day, Attie informed us if the fine weather held we girls would be employed digging over some vegetable plots for the winter planting, whilst she and Babs looked after the tearoom.

Whilst we should have been tired and restful after our busy Sunday, we were all in quite an excitable state. In the course of conversation we had the idea that, as it was our first evening together, we should take our torches and walk up to the site of the chapel. Meg suggested that it would be fun to conduct a séance; she had taken part in one before, and knew what needed to be done. It would be so exciting if we could conjure up the spirits of some long-dead monks. The boys were clearly apprehensive about this idea, but too gentlemanly to dull the enthusiasm of three keen girls. In retrospect, because Phil knew a lot more about the Island and its strange powers than we did, he probably thought it better if he and Mike accompanied us rather than leaving us to our own devices.

Chapter 8

Ghosts of the past

Eventually, the boys managed to convince us that holding a séance was not a good idea, and instead we opted to walk up to the site of the ruined chapel. I had hoped that by sitting in quiet contemplation, some Island spirits might appear to me. None of us knew the history of the chapel at this point, so the existence (or otherwise) of 'chapel spirits' could be authenticated later if we asked Attie and Babs about the chapel; omitting, of course, that we had already been there searching for spectral clues.

When Attie had told me about the chapel site on the top of the Island, I had no idea what to expect. Perhaps it would be a gothic folly with crumbling ivy-clad masonry and gaping vaults. Instead there stood, partly buried in a declivity in the grassy knoll at the top of the hill, two rounded stones, looking like small grave markers. In this respect the little lichen-encrusted stones could have proved to be a great anti-climax for me, yet tonight, whilst the sun was beginning to set and a crescent moon rising in the darkening sky, there was a strange preternatural atmosphere in the stillness of the sea and the glow of the lichens on the small marker stones.

I recalled that as we walked up the shingle path to the top of the Island, it was in perfect silence; for we were a group of friends in harmony with each other and words were neither necessary, nor appropriate. As the sun began to drop below the horizon the light changed to peach and amber and parts of the terrain seemed to irradiate, as if King Midas himself had poured liquid gold on the land. The shadows intensified and the vegetation seemed to give out a strange lime-green light; we stood in silence.

I later discovered that from this vantage point, a site known as Lamanna could be seen only a short distance away, across the water at Hannafore. Walking a little further round from the chapel, a tall ancient standing stone, believed to have pagan and ritualistic origins, could also be seen half hidden in the undergrowth and this stone was directly aligned with the Lamanna site, which had an important and direct connection with the Island chapel.

The Island chapel and the Lamanna site were both once dedicated to St Michael the Archangel. Another connected religious site not far away on the mainland, between West Looe and Polperro, was Talland Parish Church. Attie describes this church in her *Tales*[xxxi] as a parent church for the Island chapel. Talland Church, which is dedicated to St Tallanus, stands dramatically on the cliff-top and several years after I had left the Island, the sisters, ever mindful of the connection between these two holy places, bought the old pipe organ from St Tallanus Church, as progress had forced the parishioners to abandon it for a more useful electronic version.

Britain has over a thousand Islands around its coast and many have had spiritual connections, some are the final resting place of saints and holy men; however Looe Island has never been in this category. Between

1290 and 1547, the Island was known by a number of different names; including St Michael of Lamanna and St Nicholas Isle[xxxii] However from 1547 until 1748, the island was most commonly known as St Michael's Island, notwithstanding a couple instances in Tudor times, when some documents cite its name as St George's Island [xxxiii] . This old Tudor name then became part of the Islands dual English name of St George's Island and Looe Island from 1748 onwards. Whilst the See of Glastonbury did try to purloin St Michael for Looe Island, to the best of my knowledge, there are no saintly relics on there and no stories of St Michael visiting it. The same is also true of Looe Island's other holy namesakes, Nicholas and George.   Perhaps this is why for me, and the people of Looe, the Island is always Looe Island, even though the Island has the unique distinction of now having two official English names.

Lack of saints and relics notwithstanding, Looe Island has in its past been the home to holy men, who retreated from this world for prayer and contemplation. Pilgrims visited the Island because they believed that the very soil that they trod was the same place where the young Jesus might have played; it was a place where pilgrims could receive spiritual refreshment, and live a simple life away from the pressures of society. In this respect, the reasons that tourists visit Looe Island today are not dissimilar, as a short boat trip to the Island will allow you to step back a thousand years and hear nothing but the waves against the shore and the wind in the grass, carrying the breath of tranquility and spiritual contemplation, imbibed in centuries of history.

The marker stones nestled in a bed of grasses and velvet mosses. Lichens of soft green, bright orange, gold and white had painted them in a delicate palette of colours. I wondered who had placed the marker stones there and when; for they must have been carefully laid. Even now, this is an unanswered question in my attempt to re-live and re-discover that experience of 40 years ago. Nearby there were some more half-buried ancient stones, some of which had some decorative carving on them. Laid together, the soft, rounded shapes of the stones echoed the contours of the Island and the waves of the sea beyond. These partly buried stones and grassy lumps indicated that more stones were hidden beneath the grassy surface of the Island chapel site, giving a tantalizing hint of stories yet untold.

Stones marking the site of the Island chapel (Carolyn Clarke June 2013)

On many occasions Attie books tell of the strange spell of the Island. In one of her *Tales* she recounts an incident when, during a séance, she fell asleep at around the time when the friends who were with her received some kind of message from 'the other side' and went off to dig without her. The message had spelt out that treasure was buried under the lawn of Island house[xxxiv]. On receiving this message, her friends left Island House armed with spades and embarked on digging. The strange part of this story was that they all seemed to think that Attie was with them during the search. Was it really possible that some spirit had taken her place?[xxxv]

Strange phenomena, with the invariable precursor of low light and a group of people in a state of heightened excitement and anticipation, would be the rational explanation of Attie's experience, and equally it provides the logical explanation of our silence and closeness that night and the strange gold light that lit the Island; or was some greater power casting a strange spell over us? I was reminded of Shakespeare's *Tempest* and of scenes in *A Midsummer's Night Dream* and faery dust being sprinkled in our eyes.

Picking up Attie's story of the séance some 40 years later, when I talked to Sheila Ravine, she informed me that she and Gus took part in a dowsing exercise with Attie and some other friends, all of whom independently picked up signals at the same spot. When in 2008, the Time Team carried out excavations at the chapel site they were asked to use one of their diggers to excavate below the point where the diviners had tried to dig. Disappointingly, no treasure was to be found but the Time Team did unearth a very large stone, which now stands in the garden of Island House.

After a while the sky changed from red and gold to azure and turquoise, and we made our way back down to the tearoom, and a welcoming hot drink, before turning in for the night. It was on that night, whilst walking to the washroom with Meg that we saw hundreds of bats in the twilight, fluttering like tiny black sparrows, as they wheeled and circled around the path.

Bats serve as an important indicator of a healthy ecology, and their presence on the Island indicated that it was an environmentally good place to be. Forty years on I am keen to discover if these bats had been roosting in Island House or in the woodland area and whether the Island is still home to such a large colony.

Tucked up in our bunk beds Meg and I talked about our lives and discussed what we imagined the sisters would require of us in our role as Island helpers, until gradually we drifted into the arms of Morpheus.

Chapter 9

The Glastonbury Connection

The following morning I was once again woken by sun streaming through our thin curtains with a laser-like intensity, we eagerly got out of our beds and made our way over to the tearoom, and soon after breakfast I had an opportunity to talk to Attie about the Island chapel.

Attie told me that the chapel was part of the See of Glastonbury and there was a local legend that Joseph of Arimathea had left his nephew, the Christ-child Jesus, to play on the shores of Looe Island whilst he traded on the mainland. As long ago as Roman times there were established trade links between the Middle East and Cornwall, where goods such as spices and dyes, were traded for tin; therefore this beautiful legend had a sound historical basis, as Joseph of Arimathea was a merchant-trader.

Of more immediate interest to me, were Attie's descriptions of the excavation work which had begun on Hannafore point in the 1930s. The Hannafore cliff faces Looe Island, and the excavations provided archeological evidence of a church and monastery there. Attie explained that up until the last ice-age the Island was joined to the mainland, although these days it is normally only accessible by boat. However on a couple of days of the year, an unusually low tide reveals the ancient spit of land that once linked Looe Island to the mainland and at these times it is possible for the Island to be reached on foot across the rocky sea bed. This abnormally low tide would sometimes coincide with Good Friday, when throngs of pilgrims would make the journey from the church on the mainland to the Island chapel.

It was believed that Celtic monks visited the Island as early as the sixth century and a Benedictine chapel was established there around 1085[xxxvi]. The ruined chapel on Looe Island and the monastery and church that existed on the Hannafore hill site (then known as Lamanna) were both dedicated to St Michael. Attie's research had suggested that because of the difficult crossing to Looe Island in the winter, with at least two known casualties, a mainland church, looking out to the Island chapel, was established as a place for pilgrims to visit when the sea was too rough to allow for a crossing over to the Island. The mainland site was also believed to house a small monastic settlement and was larger than the Looe Island one, although originally it was believed that the two chapels were mirror images of each other.

These two early Celtic chapels would have been built of wood, and then later replaced by simple stone-built structures, before being re-vamped with architectural features, including a chancel during the twelfth century when they were owned by Glastonbury Abbey. Further evidence that these two chapels were linked was provided by the ancient marker stone on Looe Island, which was directly aligned to the Lamanna site.

At the time of my conversation with Attie much of this information was conjecture, as the Island chapel had never been archeologically excavated, Attie's assumptions being based on the excavations at Lamanna, instigated by the archaeologist C. K. Croft

Andrew in the 1930s, but cut short due to the onset of World War II. Croft Andrew's excavations were never resumed, but Attie and Babs had hoped to get the chapel site professionally dug in the future and until that time, felt that it should remain completely undisturbed. Finally Attie said that she thought that the 1930s excavations of Lamanna had shown evidence of post holes suggesting that the nave of chapel could have been an ancient structure originating back in Celtic times. It could therefore be deduced that similar findings might be found on Looe Island.

As it was already known that the Island chapel pre-dated the Lamanna church there was every chance that post holes would also be found on the Island chapel site. A small religious settlement was known to be on the Island by 1085 as two Benedictine monks, Prior Elias and Brother John had been sent over to the Island from the Lamanna settlement to form a cell (or quorum) there.

At the time when the first building was erected on the Island England had been recently conquered by the Normans and a wood, mud and thatch chapel was built there, during what was known in religious terms as the Celtic or Dark Ages. Later this was wooden structure was replaced by a simple stone chapel. An early map, which dated from the time of Henry VIII, showed this stone chapel with its thatched roof, still standing on the Island[xxxvii], indicating that the Island had an active religious community for at least 500 years.

I would have loved to have discovered more and pressed Attie further, but this was not to be, for she suddenly digressed from archaeology to strange stories of bodies found on the Island.

Tantalisingly Attie mentioned that a large skeleton with particularly long fingers had been washed up on the shores of the Island. The bones of an African man had also been found, his presence on the Island was believed to be because he had got into a fight with a feisty lady called Jochabed nicknamed 'Black Joan' by the locals. Jochabed was involved in the smuggling trade and had lived on the Island in the nineteenth century, with her parents and siblings. With the somewhat vivid imaginations of young girls, Meg, Val and I speculated as to whether when Phil had supposedly been digging the reservoir in the woodland, Attie had actually sent him off to look for burials.

Attie herself was fascinated by the Island's ghost stories, and talked about a Miss Elizabeth Steed Shapcott whose collection of stories included the fight between Black Joan and the African man. Miss Steed Shapcott's writings also included the tale of an elderly dressmaker in Looe who in 1850 stayed overnight on the Island and whilst sitting at the top of the Island felt that someone was standing behind watching her, and her fear was so great that the hairs on the back of her neck stood up and she became anxious to return back to the safety of the mainland as soon as possible. Such a story reminded me of Attie's words that although many are attracted to the Island, it also has the power to repel.

Chapter 10

The Time Team Excavations

When the Channel Four Time Team excavated the chapels of Lamanna and Looe Island in 2008 they discussed the reasons as to why Glastonbury Abbey would have changed the names of these two Cornish chapels to St Michael. St Michael was a prestigious saint, who it was thought weighed the souls of the dead when they reached the gates of heaven. As the patron saint of mariners, it would be fitting to name a sacred island after him. Additionally, the commercially minded monks of Glastonbury wished to associate all Glastonbury sites with this illustrious saint, and counteract the competition from St Michael's Mount, by claiming their own association with him.

After 1584 the Island's name changed to St George's Island[xxxviii] possibly as a result of the increasing popularity of St George as a saint. For example, during the Tudor times, when England was alternatively threatened by the French, Spanish and Scots, it is not inconceivable that St George, as the quintessential English saint, would overturn St Michael in the fervour of Tudor patriotism. Nonetheless the name change was relatively short-lived with the Island's name reverting to St Michael's Island by 1607 and retaining that name until 1748[xxxix] when it became known as Looe Island. To date I have not discovered exactly *why* the Island then took on the dual English names of St George's *and* Looe Island. Although I would guess that it could be because there was a movement to revert to the patriotic name of George, but the local people were used to calling it Looe Island and failed to completely embrace its other name.

It was thought that in those far off times one of the roles of the monks on the Island was to keep a beacon light shining in the chapel to guide ships across from the mainland, and that the chapel would also serve as a lighthouse for ships crossing those rocky waters. As I reflect on how history will often repeat itself, I am reminded of a part of Attie's memoirs when she describes how, in the early days when Babs lived on the mainland, they would communicate with each other by flashing torches to one another. Thus, as in ancient times, Babs would stand on Hannafore point and look out for the light from the Island.

I felt enormously moved to be walking on the very soil where the Child Jesus reputedly played. One of my A levels had been Religious Studies, which had included a module on the rise of Christianity in Celtic Britain, and with this information still fresh in my mind, I remembered that Joseph of Arimathea was undoubtedly an important person to Glastonbury Abbey, having planted his walking stick - grown from a twig from the Crucifixion crown - in the grounds of the Abbey. This thorn tree later grew into a bush that flowered on Christmas Day and still attracted pilgrims to Glastonbury in the first years of the twenty first century. Even in those early times, fierce competition existed between the different religious houses and factions and any place that had a Joseph of Arimathea connection would be of interest to Glastonbury.

The archaeologist Croft Andrew's excavations on the mainland chapel site in the 1930s had proved that a wall found near the Lamanna chapel, was part of a building which could have housed monks or pilgrims. The excavations also revealed that this building was two-storied, with bedrooms for two monks on the first floor. There was a large hall on the ground floor, where pilgrims would have gathered and perhaps bought food and souvenirs. Croft Andrew's findings had convinced him that a large chancel, to house the altar, had been added to the chapel nave at Lamanna around the time that the See of Glastonbury had taken over the two chapels and, as I was later to discover, this also proved true for the Island chapel.

Croft Andrew had believed that the Christian settlements on the Island and the mainland sites pre-dated the Glastonbury settlement in the twelfth century as legal documentation had shown that there were already chapels on both sites. Croft Andrew's excavations of the Lamanna site had also indicated that the Lamanna chapel had been re-built and enhanced by Glastonbury Abbey. Channel Four Time Team excavated the two chapels in 2008 and their brief was to investigate the origin, development and connection between the two chapel sites.

During their three days of excavation of the two sites The Time Team discovered that Glastonbury Abbey had added two large chancels to both of the early chapels, as part of a bid to encourage pilgrims, and their cash, to Lamanna and Looe Island, and this building took place soon after they had taken over the sites in 1144[xl]. Doubtlessly the Joseph of Arimathea connection which linked Looe Island and Glastonbury together would also have been exploited to the full.

Time Team's Tony Robinson explained that monasteries in the Twelfth Century were run rather like medieval theme parks with each Abbey competing with one another for the best relics and those all-important pilgrims, giving their money in return for the Saint's blessing and a hopefully a shorter time spent in Purgatory. The Child Jesus legend would certainly have provided kudos and cash for Glastonbury and would, as the Dig revealed, explain why they were willing to go to considerable expense to re-build and enhance Lamanna through cutting terraces into the side of a steep cliff.

The Lamanna chapel is directly aligned with the Looe Island chapel and this would be why it was built on the side of the cliff, rather than on the top, which would have been a much easier proposition in engineering terms, for, in order to support the weight of a huge stone chancel on the side of the hill, deep footings had to be dug. On Looe Island, the problem of the weight of the chancel was not connected with its position (on the highest point of the Island), but because the Island itself is honeycombed with underground caves and tunnels.

The Time Team's dig on the Lamanna site further confirmed the link between the two chapels, by discovering that steps had been cut into the cliff face, in order to allow pilgrims to climb down to the shore; and on those special days when the tide was unusually low, walk directly across to Looe Island. It must have been a very moving sight to watch the pilgrims make their journey on foot across the rocky concourse between the two chapels, when the tides revealed the 'secret pavement' hidden under the waters.

To the south-east of the island there are two circles of treacherous rocks known as The Ranney's, and the seabed below Hannafore point is full of rocks that are so rough and jagged that even a crossing at high tide would be dangerous for modern travellers. These days the Island is accessed from East Looe, yet interestingly the Time Team experts believed that in the days of pilgrimages, the Island would have been approached by going down the rocky steps at Lamanna and setting off from the shore below.

Evidence of this theory was supported by the Royal Navy divers employed by the Time Team, who discovered an area between the rocks where the sea bed is smooth and sandy and a boat could be harboured; this would allow pilgrims to make the crossing over to Looe Island by boat. It would be a difficult and dangerous crossing navigating a course between the treacherous surrounding rocks, and many pilgrims lost their lives. Nonetheless part of the philosophy of the pilgrimage was that the greater the suffering, the greater the heavenly rewards; thus the danger would be viewed by the pilgrims as an asset rather than a deterrent.

When pieces of decorated Roman amphora were unearthed by The Time Team search and the excavations revealed a reliquary, graves and the remains of much earlier Romano-British chapels built of wood and dated from before the time of Constantine the Great, the evidence that Looe Island was a special Christian site from the time of Jesus, became irrefutable. The Time Team Excavations at the chapel site of Lamanna provided a plan of the building, and the Team uncovered an early Kist (stone lined) burial below the sacrosanct; in almost exactly the same position on the Island chapel, the intact femur of a tall, adult male, possibly a saint, was found very late on into the three day dig. As I assimilated this information, I was reminded of the large skeleton that had been found on the Island shores in the mid twentieth century, and wondered if the bones in the chapel could have been a distant ancestor of the person washed up onto the Island shores, almost as if the holy person was calling his offspring home.

Other archeological evidence proving early habitation of the Island, and discovered many years previously, were two stone boat anchors. These are medium sized stones with holes through the middle, to enable rope to be threaded through and in common usage in Roman times. However, it is perhaps questionable whether these were – as suggested by the Time Team – anchor stones, as arguably the stones found were not large enough to hold even a small boat still in anything but a calm sea (the effective weight of the stone is much reduced when immersed). An alternative theory suggested by Mike Dunn is that they were more likely to be 'sink' stones used to hold submerged tubs of wine etc. in the calmer water beneath the surface of the sea, whilst awaiting collection.[xli] However, although their exact usage is subject to debate, the Time Team did identify these stones as being Roman and therefore their presence would suggest that the legend of Joseph of Arimathea visiting the Island and Cornish mainland was, after all, not so far-fetched, and the anchor stones and pieces of amphora excavated by

The Time Team, all indicate that Looe Island was part of the sprawling Roman Empire trade network.

Even before the birth of Jesus, the marker stone erected on Looe Island may have had religious or astronomical functions, or have been a waymark or a seamark, and it is fascinating to reflect that long before the dawn of Christianity, some form of ritualistic, pagan worship could have been taking place on the Island. The pagan stone being alignment with the Christian site of Lamanna does, of course, support the theory that Christianity most usually counteracted pagan beliefs and acts of worship, by assimilating them into their own religious practices.

Marker Stone aligned with the Lamanna site. (Carolyn Clarke June 2013)

Returning to the Glastonbury era of Christianity on Looe Island, I was reminded of the stones in the garden of *Island House*, believed to be from a baptismal font on the Island. Although these stones were not alluded to on the time Team programme, their presence as an elaborate font would be supported by the Time Teams' thesis that the mainland and Island chapels would have been considerably enhanced and upgraded once they became part of the See of Glastonbury.

David Clensy's *Island Life: A History of Looe Island* describes later religious developments on Looe Island from the twelfth century onwards; his book includes a list of all the Priors of the Island church during the period between 1200 -1537[xlii], written on a slate in the Sanctuary Window in Talland Church; the very same church where Attie bought her organ, and which forms part of the same parish as Looe Island[xliii].

In 1289 St Michael's Chapel on Looe Island entered another era as Glastonbury Abbey sold the property to a local landowner and the tiny monastic settlement was replaced with a chapel served by a secular priest[xliv]. The tradition of a priest serving at the chapel continued until the time of the Dissolution of the Monasteries in 1536, when the Island chapel slipped into the secular hands of the Crown. By this time, there was, in any case, little evidence of the religious life of the Island left, save for the physical presence of the building which had gradually slipped into disrepair and ruin. The final religious strand to the Island's tale was in 1588, when the Spanish Armada, from Catholic Spain, set sail for Elizabeth I's Protestant Britain. The Armada formed a menacing crescent formation dangerously near the Cornish mainland and in full sight of Looe Island.

*

Today, the chapel ruins lie buried again, but still have the power to attract modern-day pilgrims, and an interesting postscript to the excavations on Looe Island is the supposed existence of buried treasure there. The treasure map, which Attie had received in the post from the Cumbrian clergyman, who claimed that the map had been in his family for some generations, but he now wanted to return it 'home', appeared to be authentic, as it even showed the old name of St Michael's Island on it. When Attie Babs and their friends used divining rods to try and pinpoint the exact spot where the treasure was buried, the divined information concurred with that given on the map and also that given in a séance, held by Attie at Island House some days later. Attie records that she fell asleep during the séance and on waking found that her friends were enthusiastically digging at a spot under the lawn of Island House[xlv]. As requested by the Island residents in 2008, the Time Team employed mechanical diggers to this spot, and they unearthed a large standing stone, which would undoubtedly have caused the divining rods to react. However, this was all in the future, and both sisters lived out their lives with the belief that they could have resided on Treasure Island.

With regard to the buried treasure stories, there was a moment of great excitement during the Time Team investigations, when, using geophysics techniques, the *Team* hit upon a hollow chamber, lined with a neat semi-circular wall; however, the hollow chamber only turned out to be the footings for the Island flagpole. Although no treasure was secreted there, a place directly under the old Victorian flagpole would nonetheless seem to be a most auspicious place; for the hoisting of the flag to welcome Babs home and to celebrate St George's Day, feature prominently in Attie's memoirs.

A treasure map was also mentioned on the *Time Team* broadcast, only this time its origin was cited as being from America. The Time Team dig being instigated by the American viewer's letter which enclosed a copy of the map. This begs the question of whether this was the same map that Attie had received from the Cumbrian clergyman. If so, I can only presume that it was sold with the effects of the sisters when Babs died, and subsequently found its way to America. Alternatively, there could be two or more identical and seemingly authentic treasure maps. Would these maps bear up to modern forensic tests as to their authenticity? Or indeed was there an early trade in producing treasure maps? A final conundrum about the hidden treasure is the location on the map, which also accorded with the buried stone. Maybe Attie and Babs had not been the first people to use divining rods on the Island after all.

Although The Time Team investigations failed to find buried treasure, they did find evidence of other burials on the island and also a ditch running around its highest point, where the chapel is sited. The Time Team archaeologists believed that the ditch could date from the Bronze Age, because Roman artefacts were found in the surface soil and in archaeological terms, the nearer the surface an artefact is found, the more recent it is compared with what may still lie below and (as yet) remains unexcavated.

Of special interest to me was the excavation of eight Roman coins in the ditch, for under English Law, seven or more ancient coins found on a site constitute Treasure Hoard. It was such a pity that the sisters had not still been alive in 2008, to witness this tangible proof that the buried treasure, that they always believed in, really was on their Island. Nonetheless, I know that Attie and Babs would both have agreed that the *real* treasure that was unearthed on Looe Island was the advance of our understanding and knowledge of the early history and religious activities and practices, and the proof that Croft Andrew was right when he asserted that the Island was a religious and spiritual centre long before the chapel became part of the See of Glastonbury.

Looe Island at low tide: Showing Smugglers' Cottage and the close proximity to the mainland. (Carolyn Clarke June 2013)

Chapter 11

Daffodils

It was my second morning on the Island, and once again, the sun had pierced through the flimsy curtains of the hut. The sky was a lapis blue and seagulls called and screeched as they wheeled overhead and delighted in this golden day.

Meg and I made our way to the tearoom for breakfast and to report for digging with Val and Mike, whilst Phil went off to do maintenance work in the woodland. Attie escorted the four of us to a gentle sloping field near to the old tractor shed, surrounded by protective hedges and alive with bees and butterflies. The land had been previously worked, but left awhile, and grasses and weeds had now crept into the turned soil. The field was rectangular in shape and we decided that each one of us would start digging in one corner; Meg and I would start at the short side of the rectangle nearest the entrance to the field, whilst Mike and Val would work from the opposite side, with the optimistic hope that if we worked really hard, we just might meet in the middle and complete the task by sunset.

The ground proved hard and lumpy, and when I pulled my fork out of the soil, a couple of little bulbs stuck to the tines. At the time, I had no idea that daffodils were once grown and harvested commercially on the Island. However on reading Attie's *Tales from our Cornish Island* some years later, I discovered that in her early years on the Island, she and Babs continued farming daffodils However , as a result of increasingly cheap air haulage, competition from countries, such as Holland

and the Channel Islands, which eventually rendered the Island daffodil operation uneconomic.

On reflection, I am reasonably certain that we were digging one of the old daffodil fields. Perhaps Attie and Babs had now decided that it could be put to better use growing vegetables. The little bulblets that were stuck on my fork were not recognizable to me as daffodil bulbs, for in those far off days, I thought of daffodil bulbs as being big, brown, papery things that could be seen in nets in greengrocer's shops every autumn; whilst these bulbs, which were about the size of cocktail onions, had fleshy green shoots about 2 inches long sticking out from the top.

Some years later, I read Attie's book[xlvi] which described how seasons on Looe Island were different from those on the mainland. The mild climate allowed many plants to grow all year round; I realized that what I had found must have been immature bulbs, that had self-seeded in the spring. Meg was also finding a lot of these bulbs, whereas they were far less prevalent in the partially shaded area of the field where Mike and Val were digging.

In *Tales from our Cornish Island* Attie asserted that she and Babs had taken on a whole Island, complete

> "with a daffodil farm and market garden, a house and outbuildings, two cottages in a sad state of disrepair, farm buildings and machinery, an orchard, a generator, a water pump in the cliff, three boats and a boathouse"[xlvii]

To me, it seemed that maintaining the self-sufficiency of their predecessors on Looe Island, and allowing the Island to "live" again with the buildings restored and the farming tradition continued, would always be the 'Holy Grail' of the sisters' existence. The driving factors which caused Attie to move to the Island during the bitter winter of 1964/5 were the pressing need to harvest and sell the first crop of daffodils and the additional concern of planting their early seed potatoes. Looe Island is full of contradictions and one of them is that although the sea may lash and rage against its shores in winter, rendering the short boat journey there impossible for weeks at a time, on the Island itself parts of the terrain are very sheltered and warmed by the Gulf Stream, which creates a mild micro-climate where snow and frost are virtually unknown. Some species of daffodils will bloom several weeks earlier than on the mainland.

The history of market gardening and self-sufficiency on the Island probably started in seriousness in the late nineteenth century times; the Island was then owned by the Trelawny family. The Island had been bought by Edward Trelawny, the then Governor of Jamaica, in 1743 from Benjamin Salmon "for a trifling consideration".[xlviii] The Island having been in the hands of the Mayow family since the time of the Reformation, until Burthogg Mayhow had sold it to Benjamin Salmon in 1730, who then sold it on to Edward Trelawny. From this time onwards, the Island remained in the hands various branches of the Trelawny family for nearly 200 years, being leased out to tenants who farmed it as a small holding or market garden business for most of this period[xlix]. Around 1880, sycamore trees had been planted as a wind break on one side of the Island, the trees helped shelter the crops, as well as providing cover for game shooting.

As early as 1853, a tenant of the Island, William Vague, described himself as a farmer whilst supplementing his income by growing daffodils for the London market, and by the 1940s this enterprise had grown into a large commercial enterprise. The Island was now owned by Major General Rawlins[l], who, with the assistance of his gardener (who he had brought with him from the mainland) and another family, ran the Island as a market garden and daffodil farm.

Major Rawlins took daffodil farming very seriously and the Island generator filled two rooms, one of which contained glass accumulators, which he had installed for the purpose of generating D.C electricity[li], as possibly he considered that growing daffodils on a full commercial scale might require more electricity than the existing A.C generator could provide. Maybe Major Rawlins was planning the automation of some aspects of the harvesting process, or temperature control whilst the picked flowers were in storage. There are, of course, no records as to why the Major considered it necessary to install a D.C generator on the Island, and we can only speculate as to what his motives might have been.

I gathered that the Major was something of an obsessive and may possibly have been psychologically damaged by his War time experiences, from the scant descriptions I have read of him; he seemed, to have had a somewhat eccentric and possibly agoraphobic personality. Certainly Major Rawlin's obsessive, compulsive behaviour manifested itself in a number of ways: arguably it was not unreasonable of him to feel aggrieved if people tried to land their boats on his Island; but perhaps it was a little dramatic to point a gun and threaten to fire it at anyone who would not desist from entering his waters.

Following Major Rawlins' sudden death in 1947, the Island was sold to the reclusive Mr and Mrs Whitehouse, who lived there with a gardener and his wife. Mr Whitehouse continued to run the Island as a commercial daffodil centre, albeit scaled down from Major Rawlin's days. By the time that Attie and Babs bought the Island, 15 different varieties of daffodils were being grown with successive flowering seasons between Christmas and early April in many different types and colours[lii].

In the days before cheap and frequent air traffic between the UK and Europe, southerly islands, such as Looe Island, the Channel Islands and the Scilly Isles, were all able to make good money by selling early daffodils, before they became plentiful on the mainland. On reading the list of varieties in *Tales* some of the names were strange and exotic to me, whilst others were familiar friends. I felt a special thrill of excitement to discover that, the large-trumpeted, traditional bright yellow King Alfred, and the creamy white, Beersheba, both of which I grow in my own Worcestershire garden, were recorded as being amongst the original 17 species of Looe Island daffodils. Attie talked about how Beersheba was especially valued by Easter brides, due to its near-white colour and, in common with those brides, I too love its virginal delicacy and subtle scent.

Daffodil picking has formed an important part of Cornish life since Victorian times, and as recently as the 1980s, local residents and students augmenting their grants during their Christmas vacation, could be seen helping daffodil farmers with the harvest. [liii] Nonetheless, daffodil growing is not the picturesque Wordsworthian idyll that might be imagined, the harvesting always takes place at a cold, damp time of year and each daffodil only has a 'window' of a couple of days when it can be viable for picking in commercial terms. In addition, the cut flowers stems drip with a sticky sap that can produce an allergic reaction in some people and necessitate the wearing of protective clothing. It does not require much imagination to picture the stress and discomfort involved in spending hours at a time bent down in a cold wet, windswept field sorting through and picking out the 'right' daffodils; then, when the light fades and one is cold, tired and exhausted, there is no respite, as the daffodils have to be stored, tied and packed ready for the next day's shipment to the mainland.

Clearly daffodil growing is not for the faint-hearted; but, of course, 'faint-hearted' is an adjective that could never be applied to the sisters. Additionally, Attie's ability to draw just the right people to her at the right time enabled the tradition of Looe Island daffodils to continue. For when Attie moved to the Island, Ruth the daughter of some of her friends on the mainland, temporarily moved onto the Island in order to help Attie settle in. Ruth was efficient and practical in all manner of ways, in addition she knew about daffodil harvesting, and could guide Attie on matters such as the correct moment to harvest a stem[liv] (in bud and with the bud turned at 90 degrees). Having picked the daffodils, there was still the matter of storage and packing for market. Fortunately Val, wife of the Island boatman Wren Toms, knew the secrets of commercial daffodil packing and during the winter of February 1965, she showed Attie how to bunch and tie the daffodils professionally, these were then stored in the barn (later to be the Craft Centre/tearoom). Val Toms also helped Attie and Ruth pack the daffodils ready to be lifted onto her husband's boat and transported onto the mainland.

As the person living on the mainland, Babs too had an important role to play with regard to getting the daffodils to market. In an interview with David Clensy in 1999, she describes how she got up well before the first light of the morning to box the daffodils when they arrived by boat from the Island on their way to the early morning flower train at Liskeard[lv] . What a challenge that must have been to unpack the boxes of daffodils from the Island boat and load them into her car and onto the train; all before she reported in to school to undertake a demanding and challenging job as Senior Mistress.

During this interview, Babs described how she and Attie increased the original number of species of daffodils on the Island from 17[lvi] to 37. However, neither the interview or *Tales* records how much money was ever made from their daffodil farming enterprise, and it appeared to me that the ever-generous sisters probably gave away more daffodils as gifts to their friends in Surrey than they managed to sell in the

London markets. Hence their daffodil growing must be viewed more as an interesting experience rather than an important commercial enterprise and source of profit. I also remember that the winter of 1964/5 when the sisters bought the Island, was a particularly harsh one and not only was Attie in the position of having to move to the Island in inclement conditions at a time when most '50 something' women of that era would be thinking of 'slowing down', but she was also having to learn the trade of daffodil farming, and spend hours crouched down in cold fields picking the flowers before the buds opened.

Thinking of the struggle against the elements that Attie had to bear in 1964/5 reminded me that Attie and Babs faced many different challenges in their lives. As recorded in *We Bought an Island,* Attie tells the reader that the sisters were to lose their adored brothers in 1937/8. To lose two siblings within twelve months of each other, would in itself have been enough to cause many people to 'go into themselves' and suffer depression and anxiety; nonetheless the sisters were not people to see 'half-empty cups' and, even in those early years, there is plenty of evidence to prove that whatever mental and physical challenges life threw at them the sisters rose to them. A few years after I had stayed on the Island, the sturdy boathouse that had stood near the shore of the Island since Victorian times, was completely destroyed with its structure being swept away in a freak storm of 1974. Valuable equipment, including boats, a tractor and sacks of coal were all lost to the waves. Many lesser characters would have begun to bewail their 'bad luck' and question the wisdom of Island living; but Attie and Babs were resilient and the rough seas in their turn returned most of the lost coal on the incoming tides.

When the four of us dug the field it was very hard physical work, the sun was fierce and the ground dry, it was challenging, for our young ,inexperienced muscles, as there were so many grass and weed roots tangled up in the soil. Val and Mike were doing better than Meg and I because they were not wasting time fiddling around trying to separate all the tangled grass and weed roots from the soil, but were cutting off root-tangled clods with their spades and putting them in a heap before digging the clean soil underneath. Once we adopted this technique the work progressed at a faster rate. I know that Attie used to harvest seaweed to fertilize the soil and the heaps of weeds at the perimeter of the field would have composted down into good friable soil to be spread on the newly-sown young vegetables; however, I felt sorry that so many little bulblets had had to end their lives as compost.

Despite the heavy manual work that we were doing, I began to feel cold as the sunny mid-day was retreating into a cool afternoon. I reached for my cardigan and noticed that dark clouds were beginning to form in that clear sky and before too long a 'sheep's back' appeared, reflecting the patterns left in the sand by the tides as they ebbed from the shore. Meg, ever-knowledgeable on country matters, informed us that this meant rain within 48 hours, and this gloomy forecast, together with the cooler air which seemed to energize us, provided a great incentive to carry on digging whilst we could. Sadly, even our combined efforts and motivation did not succeed in getting the job completed that day.

Reflecting that 'our field' was only one of several areas that needed to be dug, I began to enumerate all the different jobs that Island living necessitated. There were hedges that required cutting and paths that needed maintaining. There was the business of planting and sowing; repairs to buildings and machinery and the perennial challenge of coaxing life out of the temperamental generator. This list did not even begin to consider the day-to-day work of running the Island as a business for tourists, and jobs such as cleaning, cooking and forward planning with regard to replenishing provisions from the mainland. Unlike the two sisters, we all had youth on our side, and yet we had struggled to dig a relatively small area of previously cultivated land. Seen in this light, what Attie and Babs had achieved in their time on the Island was truly remarkable, and that was before I even realised that every winter Attie would be doing the backbreaking work of harvesting those precious daffodils.

Some days later, when we trekked out from the tool room carrying shears and ladders in order that the hedges surrounding the old daffodil field could be cut, Attie accompanied us. Much to our surprise she insisted on going up the ladder and cutting the hedges herself, whilst we younger people just collected the trimmings and held the ladder. I will never know whether Attie wanted to be doing the cutting because she was anxious that we might have fallen off the ladder, or simply because she felt that she would probably be quicker and more efficient than we were. Either way, the hedge was cut quickly and efficiently.

Chapter 12

Pottery

The small, rippled clouds of the sheep's back kept their promise, and by dusk creatures of the damp were appearing on the vegetation, the stones on the shingle shone with a shroud of moisture and long shiny, slugs some as big as my middle finger, and delicately patterned with spots, or veils of lace, made their way across the lawn. There were delicate pink and white snails too and large toffee shelled ones, etched with black lines and looking like over-sized humbugs, their silver slime glimmering in the moonlight.

Our shed felt colder and damper that night and we both put our daytime clothes on the bunks to provide extra warmth. In the morning the rain was driving down and the sky was leaden – there would be no Island visitors today - further outdoor work was out of the question, and even Phil was grounded.

Generally, Attie was the sister who dealt with the volunteers, organizing the work schedule and lovely meals to keep us going; Babs appeared a quieter more shadowy figure, but today, it was Babs who came into her own. I can well imagine the disappointment and frustration for both of the sisters, who now had five young people eating up their precious resources, but, due to the inclement weather, were unable to give anything back in return with regard to useful work. The flimsy, unheated huts were hardly the best places to sit around in as the rain relentlessly fell, and therefore we needed to be occupied in some capacity indoors. One of the problems of rain is that despite water being such a precious commodity on an Island greedy for full water butts and storage tanks, it does not always make its appearance at a propitious time.

Nonetheless, as we were drinking our breakfast tea, Babs appeared and asked us if we would like to help her make some craft items in the pottery studio. What a heroine, and how lovely for us! At the time, I had no idea about the previous life of the pottery studio, which I just remember as being a place beyond the generator room. Years later, after Attie had published her memoirs, I learnt about the Studio's previous life as a generator building, and it is worth quoting Attie's description in full:

> The front part housed a diesel engine for generating A.C electricity. A doorway led to another room at the rear. This was about forty feet by twenty feet, one wall of which was lined with a row of large glass accumulators. Concrete blocks supported heavy beams which ran the entire length of the room and, apart from gangways, filled all available floor space…..In (Major Rawlins' day) the electrical system had been stored in accumulators in this room[lvii]

"We Bought an Island" goes on to explain that following the death of Major Rawlins and the decision of the next incumbent on the Island, Mr Whitehouse, to scale down the daffodil farming enterprise, the D.C generator was rendered redundant. At the point when Attie was taken round the Island prior to purchase, Mr Whitehouse had dismantled the D.C generator and installed a small, but efficient, Lister Start-O-Matic A.C

Generator. With her potter's eyes wide open, Attie had the vision to see that this room, with its old D.C Generator and accumulators, was wasted space, ripe for conversion into a pottery studio. [lviii]

Recalling my morning in the pottery studio, I have hazy memories of walking past a large green water butt and the sounds of rain drops bouncing into it. The Island Lister Start-O-Matic generator was situated near here, and we walked past it before entering into a large concrete space. In this space, were housed ceramics equipment; there were benches round the sides, and underneath these, dustbins full of clay. Along the walls were shelves, with pieces of work in various stages of completion. There was a throwing wheel towards one end and in the middle of the room, a good sized electric kiln.

Years later, whilst thinking about my morning in the pottery studio, my thoughts turned to the question of what Attie and Babs did with all those glass accumulators when the generator room was converted. I was fairly confident that they would not have been transported off the Island for disposal on the mainland, for both sisters loved re-cycling and reusing objects and Attie's memoirs hint that many broken (but potentially useful items) were stored, in readiness for that day when they might be put to use. On speculating about the fate of the redundant accumulators from Major Rawlin's D.C generator room, I guessed that these would probably still be housed somewhere on the Island, and was delighted to discover, during my return visit, that I had intuited correctly. A number of these ancient accumulators are indeed still on Looe Island, with future plans by Cornwall Wildlife Trust to use them as part of a display about the Island's energy[lix]

In retrospect, there were so many questions that I failed to ask at the time, for example I failed to enquire as to how Attie and Babs went about the job of organizing the conversion of the generator room into a pottery studio. Island living would have necessitated the heavy kiln being brought across the water; Considering that the sisters had already successfully coped with the trials of transporting wine making equipment and enormous pieces of furniture over in small boats, the transport of a kiln from the mainland by boat would not have unduly worried them – but nevertheless, it would have been interesting to know exactly how this mission was achieved- . Similarly, whilst Attie's memoirs mention how she enrolled in ceramics classes and through her interest, friends who had a wide experience in producing ceramics commercially, helped them set up the studio; the exact amount and type of help given by these friends and if they visited the Island from time to time and saw the extent of the sisters ceramics business, all remain undocumented.

I was fortunate in that the school I attended had a large pottery studio and an enthusiastic teacher. I loved getting my hands covered with clay, so it was a real treat to be offered this experience again. Although Attie was the person who had formally trained in ceramics, no doubt she would have soon taught Babs the craft, for both sisters were skilled potters. With her years of teaching experience, Babs was the perfect person to show us how to make small gifts, that would be of a high enough standard to sell, and that could be seen through to completion in one session.

Babs decided that we would be making pendants today. These should not prove to be too challenging, provided that we ensured that all the air was expelled from the clay. Babs gave us pieces of clay to squeeze with the heel of our hands until all the air was gone. It was a wonderful means of dissipating any residual irritation we might have regarding the rain spoiling alternative plans. The process was not unlike kneading dough when bread-making, and we soon produced workable pieces of clay to be rolled and cut into shape; it was rather like making jam tarts, except that we did not have shaped cutters, just a variety of different cutting and smoothing instruments.

Babs wanted us to be creative; I expect she felt that every piece should be a unique handmade craft rather than have the air of mass production. The next step was to choose a shape for our pendants. By a strange quirk of fate, Val and I, who were working on a bench alongside each other, decided to make fruit. I made a pear and Val an apple. Coincidentally, when I last met Val, we were young mothers who had both moved away from our birthplaces, she was living in a cottage in the Herefordshire countryside and I was living in a Worcestershire village; at that time the two counties were amalgamated as the County of Herefordshire and Worcestershire and the County badge showed apples, to represent the cider making industry of Herefordshire and pears represent the Black Pear trees of Worcestershire, with their huge fruits that stay on the tree after the autumn leaves have fallen and can be seen silhouetted against the grey, winter skies.

As I have described it, the pendant making process sounded simple enough, yet it was a lot more challenging than we first thought. Rough edges would often form in the clay once the shapes had been cut out. These edges had then to be smoothed down before piercing a hole at the top, so that cord could be threaded through and the pendant hung correctly. The hole-making process was also easier said than done, and it took all of us several attempts.

Whilst we were making our pendants, Babs was working on the wheel. It was fascinating to watch her speed and dexterity. When we had finished our own work, she told us to write on pieces of paper what colours we would like our pendants to be glazed with. Val wanted an 'apple effect' of red and green, and I opted for an equally complex colour arrangement of yellow and green with a brown stalk and russet speckles. It is a real credit to Babs that rather than crush young dreams and creativity, she said that she would see what she could do. I remember that all the pottery pendants in the Craft Centre were glazed with a single colour that varied slightly in density, showing through the natural colour of the clay in places. They were exquisitely beautiful and to use more complex multi-coloured glazing processes would surely have made the production uneconomic in terms of time and money.

Whilst in the pottery studio we all forgot both the passing of the hours and the miserable weather outside. By the time that Babs had called us to a halt for lunch the rain had stopped, and the moisture was being burnt off by the sun, causing it to rise up in wisps of white steam, and as we walked back to the tearoom a beautiful rainbow was arching over the Island.

Chapter 13

Shells, Pebbles and Gulls

The sun was shining and the earth was drying; Attie intuited that the Island might have some visitors in the afternoon, and sent us off to prepare the tearoom ready for business. Whilst we were laying tables, she kept watch through the old Island telescope, and sure enough, a boat was soon seen, bravely heading its way towards us.

Once the last visitors had left, we all took another walk up to the chapel. The rain had left the vegetation lush and green; the first stars of evening were beginning to shine through and the bats were dancing for us, no doubt excited by the bumper crop of insects brought out by the earlier rain. The moon was rising and casting a silver path across the sea and the lights of the mainland were twinkling, evoking some enchanted celestial land. As I write, I remember how many of Attie's *Tales* recalled not just the hardships of Island life, but also ethereal moments, such as these, which made the difficulties and struggle all worthwhile.

Attie's memoirs make it clear that having volunteers could be something of a double-edged sword with regard to a lot of feeding and, in the case of a small minority of volunteers, personality challenges. Some volunteers appeared to treat the experience as just a holiday, and were not prepared to work hard, whilst others were fussy eaters and demanding 'house guests'[lx]. Nonetheless, Attie was also the sort of person that when one gave to her and the Island she reciprocated with interest.

One of my lasting memories of the sisters was how they ensured that we had a really enjoyable and memorable experience on the Island, and during my stay treats included a night-time fishing trip, a morning of shopping and sight-seeing in Looe, and half a day free time to explore the Island when all she asked of us was to report on anything that looked in need of repair or maintenance.

One afternoon, Attie told us that she and Babs were expecting friends and so we would not be needed to serve in the teashop. She suggested that we used the time to just look round for any jobs that might need attention and to relax and enjoy ourselves, and I had several plans as to what I wanted to do.

Interestingly, although all five of us got on really well with each other and spent nearly all our waking hours in one another's company, on this occasion, we all chose to be on our own. Mike I knew would want to be spending more time fixing up the CB radio system that he was attempting to install for the sisters. Although I think by this time Attie and Babs had their radio phones for communication, wireless contact would have been really useful. In thinking this over, I sometimes wondered whether or not Mike did have any success with efforts to rig up CB communication; certainly the boys' hut was a sight to behold with its numerous masts and aerials giving it the appearance of a ship in sail. The gadget-loving Attie would have no doubt been thrilled by it all.

Phil, of course, would be back digging the reservoir in the wood; to him there were no boundaries between work and play and digging was a labour of love. As for the girls, I seem to remember that Val liked sketching and that Meg read a lot, or was it the other way round? No doubt they too would be walking and exploring, although I never encountered either of them during my sojourn round the Island.

Before setting off, I packed my trusty "Observer's book of Sea and Seashore" as I wanted to explore the shore areas and rock pools. Attie had also said that there was a safe bathing area near Little Island where the sea would fill up a large rock pool at low tide. I have always loved water and swimming and this love, combined with a feeling that after so many days of frugal washing, a good soak in the sea would be desirable, caused me to add a swimming costume and towel to the contents of my duffle bag. Ready to go, I headed off for the shore, from where I planned to walk round past Jetty Bay to the large rock pool, where nature had provided a safe bathing place.

As I stepped on the main beach, I was reminded that more than two millennia ago the child-Jesus was supposed to have played here alone, abandoned by his Uncle Joseph who was busy negotiating with the canny Cornish tin merchants. Some historians claim that Looe Island was the lost Island of Ictis, or Iktin, described as a tin trading centre by the historian Diodorus Siculus, writing in the first century BC[lxi] and, although there are a number of contenders for this claim, including St Michael's Mount and the Isle of Wight, there is no doubt as to the importance of tin trading in Cornwall and Devon at this time which also drew Julius Caesar to Britain in 55BC.

The story of an only child destined for great deeds being abandoned on a deserted island, owes more to Greek mythology than fact. Imposing my Twentieth Century perspective on this story, I remember thinking to myself "Would any responsible guardian really do that, and how could Joseph be sure that his precious charge would be safe on this Island?" Of course, this view of mine totally failed to take into account the notion that destiny will always override danger, and that the magic of this charmed place would surely protect the child.

The beach, as far as I could see, contained everything a beach should have; sand, rock pools, pebbles, shells. Thinking about the semi-precious stones that the sisters collected, I searched for anything that looked special enough to take back for them, but with my untrained eyes, I failed to find anything that really stood out. Of course, each individual pebble was beautiful in its own way for there were slate grey stones banded with ribbons of white quartz, milky white and pale rust-coloured pebbles, wine-coloured ones and some that sparkled with chips of mica or were speckled like birds eggs.

Carefully, I made my way over to the rocks, which were slippery with ribbons of seaweed; as I looked into some of the pools I could see tiny rain forests of seaweed in colours of brown, lettuce-green, red and even white, like miniature corals. The red seaweeds in particular were really fine and delicate, like babies' hair and nestled amongst their fronds were the jelly blobs of sea anemones, some of which were waving their many tiny arms. Various shell fish, such as limpets, mussels and tiny, bright yellow and orange snails, which are a feature of this coast, all clung to the barnacle-encrusted sides of the pools and when I focused my eyes patiently I could sometimes see miniature green crabs and transparent water shrimps. Some of the pools seemed bottomless, whilst others were shallow and allowed the sun to easily penetrate their depths, with rippling ribbons of sun and shadow playing on their sandy floors.

Although my sister and I had spent many family holidays exploring the beaches and rock pools of Wales and Devon, I think that this was probably the first time in my life that I noticed that different types of pools contained different types of vegetation and sea creatures, depending on their size and depth. In this underwater world nothing was as it first seemed, and even those pools which appeared devoid of life, contained a myriad of different flora and fauna, once your eyes rested on them for a while.

As I walked further along the rocks, I became more aware of the gulls wheeling above me. It soon became apparent that the seagulls nested quite near here, indeed they nested on the rocks of the jetty which followed round into the same pool that was supposedly 'suitable for swimming'. On moving nearer towards the rocks I began to become aware of an unpleasant fishy smell and lots of bird droppings on the rocks. This was clearly the moment to turn round; for Attie had neglected to tell me how near the gull colony the bathing pool was, and that the 'rock swimming pool' was for avian, not human, recreation.

Gingerly, I made my way back over the rocks, thankful that I had not ventured further. I was obviously lucky that day, as I have since learnt that Little Island, which is a small rocky Islet beyond the rock pool, is a nesting colony for the Greater Black-Backed Gull.

Walking back from my abortive attempt at finding the natural swimming pool, I had witnessed scenes of destruction and carnage; broken egg shells and dried up bird fetuses littered the rocks. Initially I had reflected on the irony that a few minutes earlier I was marveling at nature's beauty, and now I was seeing dead baby gulls and broken shells, as the adults unsentimentally trod on those eggs which were not their own, and also raided neighbouring colonies for their eggs and chicks.

It was a huge relief to be back to the relative safety of a sandy beach again and only then did I understand the gravity of what I had seen. The gulls were magnificent, but equally they seemed huge and menacing. Little Island[lxii] both then and now contains the largest breeding colony of Greater Black-backed Gulls in Cornwall[lxiii] and this beautiful bird is an aggressive, opportunist and fearless predator who will also steal the eggs and catches of other sea birds. At one point the sky seemed almost black with birds waiting to attack me, as a potentially threatening human being venturing too close to their nests.

Nonetheless this feisty and aggressive bird also has its own share of predators; foremost among these is the rat, which will happily feed on young birds and all types of eggs. As gulls nest amongst rocks, they are especially vulnerable to this nimble rodent. Thinking about the 'rat question', I remembered that a few days earlier, during our pottery morning, I was passing by the open door of the generator room, when I saw the pink, naked tail of a rat or mouse scuttling behind the pipes. Could this be the cause of the broken eggs and dead chicks and fetuses? On the other hand, Greater Black-Backed gulls were egg thieves themselves; my reference book had described them as 'eating anything and everything', so maybe I was blaming the rats unfairly.

Later researches lead me to look in more detail at the question of unwanted inhabitants on small islands and I discovered that the nineteenth century, the writer Wilkie Collins, who today is much more renowned for his gothic horror stories, *The Moonstone* and *The Woman in White;* also wrote a book called *Rambles Beyond Railways,* which was an illustrated travel book narrating his 1850 walking tour of Cornwall, with his artist friend Henry Brandling. In this story Collins describes the rat problem on Looe Island as follows:-

> About a mile out at sea, to the southward of the town, rises a green triangular shaped eminence, called Looe Island. Here, many years ago, a ship was wrecked. Not only were the sailors saved, but several free passengers of the rat species, who had got on board, nobody knew how, where, or when, were also preserved by their own strenuous exertions, and wisely took up permanent quarters for the future on the terra firma of Looe Island. In process of time, and in obedience to the laws of nature, these rats increased and multiplied exceedingly; and, being confined all round within certain limits by the sea, soon became a palpable and dangerous nuisance. Destruction

was threatened to the agricultural produce of all the small patches of cultivated land on the island. [lxiv]

Collins then continues to describe how the rat problem on Looe Island was solved by the people of Looe going on to the Island and hunting them down before eating them 'smothered in onion' and with 'vindictive relish'[lxv]

Mike Dunn's book *The Looe Island Story*[lxvi] supports Collins' theory that rats probably invaded Looe Island from a shipwreck, but notes that the facts of the 1809 wreck of *The Rose*, cited by Collins as the culprit, do not match up with some of the details given in *Rambles Beyond Railways,* as there were no (human) survivors on the shipwreck of *The Rose*. Mike Dunn's book[lxvii] gives a selected list of shipwrecks on Looe Island and none can conclusively be said to be the one that introduced the rats; if indeed these invasive rodents did indeed arrive by means of boats in the first place; for rats are good swimmers and could easily have swum across from the mainland or crossed over on the rocky pavement at times of low tide. Interestingly, Dunn notes, citing the Nineteenth Century Looe historian Thomas Bond, that one of the Island's eighteenth century Smugglers, 'Mewstone Man' Finn, was also partial to cooked rat. Indeed human consumption of rats was not unknown in the UK in centuries past.

A recent biography of Jane Austen's life records that Jane's fifteen year old brother Frank set sail for the West Indies on board the *Perseverance,* and whilst writing to Jane informed her that there were so many rats aboard their sister ship the *Crown* that "the sailors caught them with fish hooks, stabbed them with forks and ate them"[lxviii] Additionally, a recent visit to an historic gaol reminded me that it was not uncommon for prisoners to keep and fatten up rats for later consumption[lxix]. Clearly folk in the eighteenth and nineteenth centuries were less precious about what they ate than their modern counterparts are.

In addition to eating rats, 'Mewstone Man' is also cited as eating rabbits that he caught on Looe Island[lxx]. As I did not find any evidence of rabbits during my stay on the Island I can only assume that, because rabbit meat far more acceptable to modern taste than rat, the Island conies had all been eaten long ago by the its human residents[lxxi].

Whatever agency introduced the rats, it can be categorically stated that the success of the festive cull to eradicate these rats was short-lived. Attie mentions rats a number of times in *Tales* and despite the sisters owning several pet cats and dogs, the rats continued to multiply and were continuing to give problems into the 1990s, as the author David Clensy recalls :-

> When I stayed at Smuggler's Cottage in the mid-1990s, it was in a dreadful state broken glass in some of the windows, rats under the floorboards and the bed was sodden with damp in the back room - I used to sleep on the sofa in the front room.[lxxii]

On 22 January 2013 the *Western Morning News reported* that rodent control work, to safeguard birds' eggs and their chicks, had been in place for 15 years on

Scilly's uninhabited islands. As a result of this initiative, the Islands are now rat-free and rodent control has been extended to some of Scilly's inhabited Isles. Cornwall Wildlife Trust also initiated its own rat eradication programme for Looe Island. Following a feasibility study in 2004 the programme was implemented in 2006. The first stage was the removal and careful management of domestic waste, accompanied by monitored baiting. By the end of the winter of 2007 the problem had been dealt with and to date (August 2013) Looe Island is rat-free. Clearly these anti-rodent measures are a lot more successful than ingesting rats with fried onions, but nonetheless, rats are very clever opportunists and the Island is still monitored in case they decide to reappear.

Chapter 14

Excursions

July turned to August and the days continued to drift by, until one morning Attie asked us if we would like an excursion to the mainland to collect provisions and walk around Looe. Strangely enough, whilst my memories of my days on the Island are largely intact, this particular morning, remains unmemorable; possibly because I had sent my heart on souvenir shopping and failed to focus on the beauty and quaintness of Looe itself.

I think that all five of us went over on the boat to the mainland, but I cannot be certain, it could have just been us three girls. I do not even remember if I looked round Looe alone or with the group, or even what I did apart from wandering round a few shops, as many teenagers do, in a desultory manner.

I recall feeling closed in by the jostling crowds of holiday makers thronging the narrow streets of East Looe. The souvenir shops all seemed to sell roughly the same sorts of goods, and these mementos failed to inspire me in the way that the sisters' crafts had. I was physically detached from the Island, yet it still seemed to be exerting its magnetism and pulling me back. Stepping onto the shores of Jetty Beach some hours later felt like coming home again, and coincidentally my permanent home was nestling in the Island mailbag in the bottom of the boat, for the bag contained a letter from my Mother.

Up until her last years, Mum was always a prolific writer, who generally preferred to put her thoughts on paper than pick up the telephone. I loved receiving her letters, and this one was no exception. Mum relayed all the family stories in her usual compressed, breathless way. Dad and sister keeping well; Granddad, still in hospital; must be on the mend as asking for a drop of whiskey. It was good to hear from home yet, as had been the case on my excursion to Looe, the world beyond the Island seemed strangely remote, I was part of it, yet separate. The West Midlands were another life; another world and so was East Looe with its ancient, winding streets and busy crowds.

*

Not long after the morning in Looe, Attie had arranged for us to go mackerel fishing with Wren Toms, the boatman who had rowed me over to Looe Island, and one of Attie's many friends from the fishing fraternity. It was a black and moonless night and, because mackerel need deep water, the fisherman drove the vessel out some distance away from the shore. The water was dark, still and silky. It looked freezing cold and despite wearing virtually every stitch of clothing that I had with me, I shivered slightly as I watched Wren unravel the orange nylon feather line and deftly let it run through his fingers. He let us all have a go and told us that we would feel a tug when the fish bit and then we must pull in the line, which we did, with varying degrees of success.

There was something fascinating about the way that the fish seemed to be attracted to the line even though there was no bait attached. Even today, it still remains something of a puzzle to me as to why mackerel, and only mackerel, were attracted to the line. In those days, stocks of mackerel (and most other native fish) were much more abundant around the Cornish coast than they are today and the line method of fishing meant that there was no wastage; small fish were thrown back in the waters – everything that was taken out of the sea was for eating – nothing died in vain.

As I looked back towards the Island, wondering if I could make out any familiar landmarks in the darkness, I became aware of a strange light appearing where the boat had disturbed the waters. The light was different to that cast by electric lights or the moon; almost green in hue. Then Wren said that it was phosphorescence. When reading about it the next day, my Observers' [lxxiii]book informed me that the phosphoric glow is caused by the action of a boat disturbing microscopic plankton causing them to emit a brief, bright light; similar to the glow of glow worms and caused by a similar chemical reaction.

Once our eyes have been open to sights we will often see them again. I have since encountered sea phosphorescence on a number of occasions, including during a moonlit boat trip on The Nile, but never has the glow been as bright, or the waters so dark, as it was in those Cornish seas in 1971.

Whilst Wren opened my eyes to the ghostly nighttime glow of primeval plankton, it was Val who opened my eyes to the beauty of mackerel, which I previously only saw as copper coloured, flattened edibles that we sometimes ate with salad. Val pointed out the many different colours on the mackerels' body picked up by the boat's lantern, pinks, yellows and greens, which reflected and refracted on the pearlescent body of the fish. The underside of mackerels are banded with blue-black ripples, which reminded me of cloud formations before the rains and the rivulets left on the shore as the tide retreats. Having closely examined these beautiful creatures, Val decided that there was no way that she could cook and eat them, and Meg and I caught in the same sentimental moment, decided likewise. To my shame and embarrassment, we left the two boys to take up the bucket of fish to Attie and Babs whilst we went straight to bed, without even thanking them for making such a magical evening possible.

Living on Looe Island would eventually change me in many, almost imperceptible, ways but, in common with the heroes and heroines of legends who were washed ashore on enchanted isles, I too had lessons to learn first. With the eyes of an adult, I can see that our behavior was tactless and immature; how much better it would have been to have brought the fish to Attie, and thanked her for allowing us to take part in the fishing expedition. Looking back, we could have just said that we were not hungry, or that we wanted the sisters to have all the fish for themselves. Instead, the fishing trip has always been slightly tainted for me by the way that Attie was so cross and hurt by our behaviour and had no compunction in telling us so the next morning. Of course, we were all extremely sorry and soon forgiven, but the memory of our ungrateful behaviour remains as a life-lesson that will, on occasions, return to haunt me.

Chapter 15

Smugglers

Smuggling became rife in Cornwall during the late eighteenth century. The cost of the Anglo-American War of Independence and the Napoleonic Wars had forced the debt-ridden government to impose and increase Customs and Excise duties on a number of luxury goods. Spirits, tea, lace and salt, were all heavily taxed and, whilst these long and costly wars impacted on all parts of the country, they hit the Cornish economy particularly hard. The tax on salt from Brittany and Spain was up to 40x the cost of this commodity in peace time. The Cornish fishermen were, in those times, reliant on high quality salt to preserve their pilchard catches; therefore this tax was a particularly cruel one, as pilchards were one of Cornwall's largest exports.[lxxiv]

Driven by hunger and an independent spirit, the fishing community of Cornwall turned to smuggling and this trade formed an important part of the local economy. As the war with France intensified, smuggling became a serious drain on the exchequer and anti-smuggling measures became ever more draconian and sophisticated. Nevertheless, these measures were no real match for the wily smugglers. For example, Zephaniah Job of Polperro[lxxv] had far-reaching connections with those engaged in the smuggling trade; connections which even extended to acting as banker to the smugglers and issuing his own banknotes. Additionally, due to the support, sympathy and collusion of whole communities in the late eighteenth and early nineteenth century, it was said that no Cornish jury would ever find a smuggler guilty[lxxvi]

Looe Island's smuggling activities have always been inextricably linked in my mind with the caves on its west side, these caves are only accessible by sea and look out onto the cliffs and sparsely populated Rame Peninsula and road up to Hannafore Point. Looe Island's smuggling past is reinforced by its aptly named *Smugglers' Cottage* and tales of secret hiding places in the old cottage and barn. As I look at my photograph of the largest of the Island's caves, I recall Attie's story of her treasure map; curiosity whetted, I go to the Internet to find out more. One unattributed article states that:-

> On the 15th of September 1900 *The Cornish Times* reported that 'Remarkable discoveries at Looe Island' had been made'. The report told the story of two young men who had become enthralled with stories of smuggling and treasure while staying in Looe on holiday these gentlemen (named as Messrs R. Lawson, of the Inner Temple, and F.A. Somers, F.S.A.) approached Sir William Trelawny for permission to visit the island to investigate further. [lxxvii]

The same Internet-posting notes that:-

> A cave was soon found, and shortly after an adjoining one. The style of their 'architecture' was said to be that of a very early pre-mesopelagic or Etruscan design (around 800BC), similar to the Etruscan caves at Clusia

in central Italy. It was decided to make further excavations, and the most remarkable results were obtained. At a distance of about 18ft below the surface, St. George's Island was nothing but an extensive ramification of caves. Everything pointed towards the fact that these caves were originally above the ground, as many of the larger ones - of which there were said to be dozens - were built of brick, similar to that used on the Hannafore Estate and probably obtained from the same source. The caves were evidently very ancient, probably prehistoric structures, several having collapsed over their long history. (Additionally), claims of submerged networks of man-made caves, which may have been used for hiding contraband to collect at a later date, have also been made[lxxviii]

Photograph showing one of the caves used by the Island smugglers and reputed to contain buried treasure. (Carolyn Clarke circa 1970)

As with many stories connected with Looe Island, the ending is bemusing and enigmatic. The *Cornish Times* neglected to publish a follow-up account, and the story only reached its tantalising conclusion in 2008 when The Time Team investigated the chapels on Lamanna and Looe Island. The Etruscan caves on the Island were mentioned in the programme, as evidence of how far back the Island's history stretches; nonetheless it was concluded that, even today, it would be an impossible feat of engineering to construct underground passages linking Looe Island with the mainland,[lxxix] thus the secret hideaways must be seen as the product of journalistic exaggeration, which could not be substantiated. This would also explain why the *Cornish Times* had no interest in printing a follow-up story.

Whilst a complex cave network for hiding contraband remains little more than a journalistic fantasy; Smugglers - or more correctly, in the case of Looe Island, receivers and disposers of commodities smuggled out from the Channel Islands and the Continent, without paying HM Customs and Excise their cut – were a crucial part of Looe Island's history in the eighteenth and nineteenth century.

Cornish Smugglers have caught the imagination of journalists and historians for well over 200 years, and in terms of fame and notoriety, the only Looe Island inhabitants that could ever match Attie and Babs were the brother and sister team Amram and Jochabed Hooper. The Hooper siblings were the last of a line of Island Smugglers who operated between the 1790s and mid-1840s, their parents, Anthony and Elizabeth, rented a property[lxxx] on Looe Island from the Trelawney family.

The Hooper family was closely linked to the Finn family, who also inhabited the Island during this time. Currently Barbara Birchwood-Harper, curator of Looe Old Guildhall Museum, is conducting a detailed research project on the Smugglers of Looe Island, and my version of the Island's two most famous Smugglers must therefore be read as a brief and simplified version of the complex relationships and activities of the Smugglers of Looe uncovered in her research. Readers interested in this aspect of the Island's history are advised to look at Mrs Birchwood-Harper's work. [lxxxi]

The Looe Smugglers organised their activities around ships that unloaded contraband goods onto the island, mainly from Guernsey and France, up to the time of the Napoleonic Wars in 1815, and thereafter just Guernsey, as after the start of the wars, the French became unreliable and wont to give the Coastguards tip offs. The role of the Smugglers of Looe Island was to hide and store the smuggled goods in safe and secret hiding places on the Island.

On receiving a signal from the mainland, which informed them that the coast was clear, the Looe Island smugglers would then row the goods out to various places on the shore and up river[lxxxii] . In her article, *A Nest of Smugglers,* Barbara Birchwood Harper refers to one of the earliest sources of information about the Island Smugglers, *The Old Smuggler's Tale* (1899) in which Commander H.N. Shore – later Lord Teignmouth - published an interview with an elderly former smuggler who called himself William Penaluna.

Penaluna's stories cover the 1830s in particular and feature a vessel called the "Daniel & William" which plied her free trade between Guernsey and Roscoff (in France) and the Cornish coast. Penaluna mentions Looe Island, and its inhabitants "Hamram" Hooper and his daughter 'Tilda. William Penaluna's tale describes how 300 tubs of spirits were dropped on Looe Island and then hidden by the Hoopers in secret hideaways, known only to the family and that it was 3 months before the goods could be distributed[lxxxiii].

The *Old Smuggler's Tale* clearly shows that the smugglers' role in the organised illegal activities on Looe Island would be to receive and hide the smuggled goods. With regard to the logistics of this, the Looe Island smugglers would load the smuggled goods into small boats, and, in the same manner as the pilgrims of old, steer the laden boats around the dangerous rocks surrounding the Island and into the caves on the west side, where they would stay until it was safe to hide the goods on the Island itself, ready to be rowed out to the mainland.

In an age when record keeping was less reliable, and in dealing with an occupation where secrecy and the covering of tracks was important, there is some ambiguity about the Island smuggling community in terms of origins and relationships. A problem compounded by the destruction of the Trelawny papers during the Blitz. Nonetheless, what is known is that Looe Island had two separate families, the Finns and the Hoopers, living there during part of the eighteenth and nineteenth centuries.[lxxxiv] The Finns' time on Looe Island pre-dated the Hoopers by about 40 years; John Finn having been recorded as living on Looe 1781/3[lxxxv].

The Finns originated from Mewstone and John Finn was known as the "Mewstone man". John Finn's story is both fascinating and puzzling, for Mewstone is a tiny rocky Island off the coast of Plymouth and local legend has it that he was banished there by the locals[lxxxvi], for being a nuisance to his neighbours. Mewstone is much smaller than Looe Island. There have never been any trees growing there to provide fuel, and no underground springs to yield fresh water, yet Finn appeared to enjoy living on his lonely Mewstone, which clearly gave him a taste of island living.

It was believed that during Finn's sojourn on Mewstone, food was shipped out to him by locals, but I have not discovered any details about this. Did the locals just leave the food and depart or did they interact with Finn? Was he allowed a boat or was he absolutely marooned on the Island as part of his punishment? After 7 years of living on Mewstone, Finn and his family, who lived on the Plymouth mainland, moved to Looe Island.

Public records describe the Hooper family as fishermen, but their fishing income was augmented by the lucrative nineteenth century trade in smuggled goods. Using the Hooper family Bible, Barbara Birchwood-Harper, has shown that the Finn and Hooper families were possibly linked through intermarriages, as both families had used the Bible and George Finn, the son of 'Mewstone' John, had inscribed pious and tantalising entries at the top of the inner covers.[lxxxvii]

Amram and Jochabed were christened Philly and William, in the parish of Talland, where the baptismal record gives details of their godparents which included a clergyman's relatives and two gentlemen, and would give credence to the notion of the siblings originating from an aspirational, upper middle class background. One Internet source describes Amram's family as having been 'superior people', most likely of the upper middle class, who were punished for some state offence.

Amram was in a college of learning at the time of this punishment and his whole career was wrecked. Therefore it can be conjectured that when his family moved to Looe Amram's new career as a smuggler might have been carried out in the spirit of revenge against the injustice of the law of the land. A local fishermen, employed to fish with Amram said, when asked by his wife what they talked about, "*his words were few, but pure silver every one of 'em*".[lxxxviii] Such an assessment of Amram indicates an intelligent man, who always kept his own counsel, and for this reason, it is unlikely that we will ever really know why the son of a 'superior family' decided to turn to smuggling.

The names Amram and Jochabed came from the Old Testament. *A Nest of Smugglers'* describes how one of their descendants, Mary Philp, lent the author their Family Bible, and she noticed that the page in Exodus, where the names were cited, was marked with a bay leaf that had left a faint mark on the text.[lxxxix]

Amram and Jochabed's mother was Elizabeth; (nee Venning) had been previously married to a Mr Benjamin Christopher, by whom she had three children, one of whom, Benjamin, was drowned in a fishing accident, in Plymouth. Jochabed and Amram's father was Anthony Hooper and it is likely, but by no means certain, that he originated from Morval in the parish of Liskeard [xc].

"Mewstone Man" John Finn, also had a daughter called Elizabeth, and as this daughter and Elizabeth Hooper, are both recorded as having come from Plymouth. It was believed at one time that it was this Elizabeth who had married Anthony Hooper; however, in truth this is very unlikely. In the first instance, the dates of Elizabeth Finn's children's births do not agree with those of Elizabeth Venning/Christoper/ Hooper. A much more likely explanation of Elizabeth Hooper's origins is provided by Mike Dunn, who suggests that Elizabeth Christopher, who was by then, a widow, was living in the Looe area at the time, and was befriended by the Finn family. After joining the Finn family on Looe Island, Elizabeth Christopher married Anthony Hooper, and Amram and Jochabed were two of their children[xci].

Amram and Jochabed lived in a rambling farmhouse (subsequently demolished) on the Island and it was said that there was hidden treasure from smuggled goods under the farmhouse floors[xcii]. During the early part of the twentieth century, some visitors to the Island fell through the floor of a cowshed, which could have been a storage place for the smuggled goods[xciii]. Other theories as to where the contraband may have been hidden include under the window seat in *Smugglers' Cottage*[xciv]

Amram and Jochabed obtained notoriety whilst living on Looe Island, and the locals of Looe nicknamed Jochabed 'Black Joan', whilst Amram had the nickname of Finn[xcv]. Black Joan was the more violent of the two, and the murder of a Negro, whose skeleton was found on the Island, is attributed to her[xcvi]. Local gossip has it that Joan adopted a male persona, not only in her dress, but as a bare knuckle fighter, who smoked a pipe. The siblings also devised a unique signalling method to warn Smugglers of the whereabouts of Revenue officers. A smuggling colleague called Fidick would ride his white horse along the mainland coast (facing the island) and, if he remained in the saddle, all was well, but when he dismounted, this meant trouble. A pre-arranged signal, of lights or flags, would be passed by the residents on the Island to the Smugglers in their craft, waiting out at sea.[xcvii] Barbara Birchwood-Harper, who interviewed a descendant of Fidick, has also verified this story, and further evidence of messages being passed from the Island to the mainland can be found in a court account in April 1815. During this hearing, Richard Cook was tried at the Cornwall Assizes charged with lighting fires further up the coast on the cliffs at Rame Head, in order to warn the Smugglers that Revenue men were in the area. Jochabed herself was a mistress of trickery, and would seek the coastguard's help to rescue her ailing boat, therefore, in effect, acting as a decoy and diverting them from watching out for Smugglers.

By the mid nineteenth century Cornish smuggling activities had declined, this was due to a number of factors, such as the formation and growth of a well-paid and professional Customs and Excise service that would try cases in London rather than locally. Additionally peace, prosperity and the industrial revolution (with demand for Cornish tin and copper rising by the day) all helped quench the fire of hunger and starvation. Finally, smuggling was no longer a lucrative trade. A period of peace and prosperity had resulted in the lowering of Customs and Excise Taxes, with the death knell being struck by Peel's 1842 and 1845 Free Trade Budgets, which slashed import taxes and caused smuggling to become uneconomic compared with the rich pickings of the previous decades.[xcviii]

By the late nineteenth and early twentieth century the only money to be made from smuggling was through tourism, and the publication of smuggling memoirs. In 1928 Miss Elizabeth Steed Shapcott, a founder member of the Old Looe Society, published a collection of stories about the Island, amassed through interviewing several elderly local people who remembered Amram and Jochabed in their smuggling days. Miss Steed Shapcott's observations were, in all likelihood, the source of the image contemporary readers have of Jochabed Hooper wearing manly attire, and having a feisty demeanour[xcix]. Whilst Jochabed's clothes might evince comment from a middle-class Edwardian lady diarist, in truth it is hardly strange or surprising that she would be dressed in a practical and 'manly' way[c] as she was living a working life on an island, and involved in the largely male world of smuggling. Today Miss Steed Shapcott's writings have provided readers with a wealth of information and colour in respect to life on Looe Island in Victorian times; her interest in apparitions, the supernatural and Black Joan were noted earlier in the Island ghost stories, and in the tale recounted by Attie, of Jochabed's fight with a large-boned negro man, whose remains were later found on the Island.

An interesting postscript regarding Miss Steed Shapcott's observations is that she shares the name of Shapcott with Amram's daughter-in-law, Fanny Shapcott Honey, of West Looe, who married Amram's eldest son, Benjamin. I wonder if a genealogical search might show these two women, who clearly shared an interest in smuggling families, are thereby possibly related, for even today, Looe is a close knit community and there are a number of surnames specifically associated with the area, hinting at a common ancestry amongst a sizable proportion of its inhabitants.

Another Island character of the 'smuggling era' on Looe Island was Thomas Fletcher, an Irishman, who came to Looe as a coastguard and who moved to *Smuggler's Cottage* (briefly re-named *Coastguard's Cottage*) in the 1830s, in order to keep an eye on activities on the Island. Fletcher, married a local woman, raised a large family and in the best traditions of 'Gamekeeper turned Poacher' used his knowledge of the workings of the coastguard to aid and abet Amram and Jochabed in their nefarious deeds.

A further famous island inhabitant and smuggler was 'Tilda, also known 'Island Til' or 'Black Til', who was believed by some to be Matilda Bartlett, a woman living on the Island with the Hooper household in 1841; to confuse matters further, the Hoopers also had a daughter (born 1825) called Matilda, and others, including William Penaluna (quoted in Shore's Old Smuggler's Tales), believed that this Matilda was the real 'Black Til'[ci] . However, to date, there is no evidence to implicate either of these Matildas' in the smuggling trade [cii] .

The 1841 Census records Amram as being married to Philipa, a local lady from Looe and the 1851 census shows them to be living in Back Street Looe[ciii] with their children. Clearly, the name Benjamin had not proved to be a lucky one for Amram, for a generation after his half-sibling Benjamin Christopher was drowned in a fishing accident, he lost his own first-born son Benjamin, who died aged only two. As for Jochabed she latterly adopted a respectable life-style, marrying and living 'a quiet and industrious life'[civ]

After Amram and Jochabed and their families had left the Island, the 1851 Census Return records William and Jane Vague[cv] and their daughter Ann, who had been born on Looe Island on 4th April 1851, and Jane's mother, together with a farm servant, as all being resident there, and probably all sharing the farmhouse where the Hoopers had lived. Additionally, John Connor a Commissioned boatman and his son, lived in a temporary watch-house on the Island.[cvi] John Connor's stay on Looe Island was relatively brief, and both he and his son had left before the 1861 Census. However, although we do not have a clear record as to the exact duration of their sojourn on Looe Island, we do know that John Connor was posted there to keep a watch out for smuggling activities. It must therefore be assumed that by 1861, smuggling activities on Looe Island had largely ceased.

By the time of the 1861 census Ann Vague had four young siblings and her widowed grandmother was no longer living with the Vague family on Looe Island. However, we know that Jane Vague's mother was still alive, as ten years later her name is recorded in the 1871 Census as living on mainland Looe with her son-in-law, her daughter and their three youngest children. Along with the majority of the Island inhabitants after the smuggling era, the Vagues were farmers who augmented their income and diet through fishing, and just quietly lived out their lives. They were clearly modestly prosperous people, as William had increased his farming acreage from the 15 arable acres of Looe Island, to 30 acres on the mainland by 1871.

Apart from *Island House* being built in the 1870s, and trees being planted when Sir William Lewis Salisbury-Trelawny took possession of the Island, there was very little change in daily Island life, as different families (the Nicholls in the 1881 Census and the Walters in the 1891 Census) looked after Looe Island for the Trelawny family in the nineteenth century.

Chapter 16

The Past

It was my last night on the Island, Meg had already gone home, and in less than twenty four hours, it would be just Phil and the sisters left to await the arrival of the next batch of volunteers. As I lay in the little bunk bed, watching the sky deepen and listening to the waves swishing against the shore, my thoughts drifted to those people who, in their different ways had shaped the Island's history.

Looe Island provided a home for people since the dawn of Christianity; those who lived there had cultivated its soil and fished its waters. Between these periods of habitation, the Island had spells of emptiness, when it was reclaimed by nature. One of these empty periods was during the time of the planned invasion of England by the Spanish Armada in 1588. England was now a Protestant country, and the Island's religious community had been disbanded and nobody lived on Looe Island then, to witness the sound of the cannon balls being fired from those mighty galleons. Four years earlier the Island's name had changed from St Michael's Island to St George's Island and I wondered if it was during this fiercely patriotic time, that the name of St George's Island was seen as a rallying call to the Cornish people. The attack by the Spanish Armada is described in detail in a number of books about the Island[cvii] and an early map [cviii] shows the Armada adopting a defensive crescent formation slightly south of the Island. As in the case of the china owl, and the masonry from the chapel, the tides chose to give Attie and Babs a present from the past in the form of several cannon balls, which Attie believed could well have been fired from the Armada. Less romantically, experts believe that these cannon balls were much more likely to have been from Turkish raids along the Cornish coast[cix]. Nonetheless, as Attie noted in her memoirs, the story of the Spanish cannon balls was an engaging one, that she liked to recount to the many schoolchildren who visited the Island.

Later on in its history, the Island was mistaken for a battleship and fired at by the Germans during World War II. As a consequence of this attack, a large crater was created by a parachute mine in the wooded part of the Island; the blast broke most of the windows on the Island and even shattered some on the mainland, but fortunately the Island was unoccupied, the lack of residents doubtlessly being connected with wartime security measures. The BBC radio broadcasts took great delight in taunting the enemy with questions of "what happened to the raider who tried to sink HMS St George?"[cx] . The episode would have been particularly embarrassing for the Germans, as parachute mines were very costly, and their usage normally restricted to important military installations and targets; not uninhabited Islands!

The Atkins sisters proved to be tough and, some might say eccentric, custodians of Looe Island[cxi], yet arguably Island living could never be the terrain of the timid or conventional; the strength of character and determination necessary for coping with day to day life on the Island is evident throughout Attie's memoirs. As the new custodians of the Island in 1964, the sisters acquired some degree of fame. Following its publication in 1976, *We Bought an Island* was reviewed in several national newspapers, and a sizable illustrated article about the Atkins sisters, appeared in *Woman's Realm*. The fame of the sisters was also, in no some measure due to their friendliness and hospitality, for as they opened up their Island home to visitors, Looe Island, with its rich history and ecology, became widely known beyond the boundaries of Cornwall itself.

By contrast, some of the sisters' more recent predecessors had been reclusive with strange and eccentric behaviour patterns. Mr and Mrs Whitehouse, who were the sisters' immediate predecessors, lived on the Island with their gardener and his wife. Attie's knowledge of the couple and their plans to sell the Island - no longer in the hands of the Trelawny's - came through their gardener on one of his visits to the mainland. Attie and Babs were at the time living in Bassett Court, West Looe. The Whitehouse's themselves rarely ventured off the Island and did not receive visitors; when provisions were needed they sent their gardener over to Looe to get them. By one of the many quirks of fate that seemed to follow Attie throughout her life, she was introduced to the Whitehouses' gardener just at the moment when they had decided to sell up and move back to the mainland.

Aside from his reclusiveness, there are two other facts worth mentioning about Mr Whitehouse. Firstly, there was his anxiety about the future of the Island, a mantle which Attie and Babs later took up. During the sale of the Island Attie had been informed that it was extremely unlikely that she and Babs would be allowed a viewing. However, as Attie herself has frequently remarked, Looe Island has a power to attract and repel; although Mr Whitehouse had never met Attie before, something must have indicated to him that she and Babs were the rightful heirs. Attie and Babs were invited onto the Island and became acquainted with the Whitehouse's. Any residual doubts that Mr Whitehouse may have had regarding whether or not he should sell his island to the sisters, were swept away when he met them; for he must have intuited that the Island would be safe in their hands. Attie and Babs were therefore able to buy the Island in the face of higher bids that they could never have matched. Many years later, Attie and Babs in their turn, also rejected lucrative financial offers from developers, thus fulfilling Mr Whitehouse's belief that the Island would be safe in their hands. To quote Babs:-

> I think the island should always be owned by people who want to keep it as it is. And that's why I'm so very anxious that it will not get into the hands of private people who want to exploit it in any way, and that it belongs to a trust that has the same ideas as Attie and I had when we started.[cxii]

Reading Attie's memoirs, gave me an image of Mr Whitehouse as someone who was shy and reclusive, yet fond of animals and fiercely protective of his Island home. Reclusiveness aside, the sisters also shared these characteristics, although there were some differences, for their love of animals was conventional, in so far as their favourite pets were cats and, of course, their beloved dogs; by contrast, Mr Whitehouse had a special love of monkeys.

On the main walls around *Island House*, one can find, peeping through the ivy, weather-worn forms of lichen-covered, gargoyle-like creatures. The figures are truncated at the waist, have big ears and ape-like faces, they are lined up in a row along the wall. The gesture of a thumb under their chin gives these primates a slightly comic, contemplative air. The monkeys were added to the outside wall of *Island House* by Mr Whitehouse, in the same way that some people may choose to adorn their gardens with statues of dogs and cats.

David Clensy, who worked as a volunteer on Looe Island in the 1990s, tells us that hidden in the woodland behind *Smugglers' Cottage* are the remains of monkey huts, dating from the Whitehouse's time on the Island. Clensy recounts how on a cold day, during one of the Whitehouses' very rare excursions to the mainland, Mr Whitehouse had left the monkeys in their hut with an oil stove to keep them warm. Sadly one of the monkeys knocked this stove over and they were all burnt to death.[cxiii] Interestingly today, monkey's still live in Looe, but now they are safely nurtured in the Looe Monkey Sanctuary, which was started in the 1980s[cxiv]

One of the Ivy clad monkeys along the wall of *Island House* (Carolyn Clarke June 2013)

Mr and Mrs Whitehouse had lived on the Island since 1957, having bought it from Major Rawlins, who had lived there since 1947. Both incumbents were reclusive, but unlike Major Rawlins, they did not resort to the extreme measure of a shotgun to warn off trespassers. Clearly any one capable of master-minding the installation of the D.C generator, in order to garden the Island on an industrial scale, must be highly intelligent, but Major Rawlin's paranoia about visitors would also suggest that maybe he was mentally dislocated by his wartime experiences. In another, later age, he would have received the help and treatment he needed, but in the 1940s and 1950s he was left alone with his generator and daffodils and nobody dared venture too close to Looe Island.

Of the other twentieth century Island inhabitants, there are few people alive who are old enough to remember them and tell their tales. The problem of finding information about the inhabitants of Looe Island during the 1920s and 1930s is exacerbated by the fact that the Trelawny papers, containing records of tenancies of the island, were destroyed in the Blitz on Plymouth and Exeter, sometimes all we know are their names from the Census Returns. It is to be assumed that these Island residents were ordinary people who simply marked time farming the land and fishing the seas. Nonetheless, the different lengths of tenure have caused me to speculate on the veracity of the Island's powers to attract and repel.

Mr and Mrs Topman, bought the Island in 1921, but only stayed there a few months[cxv], whereas the Hoopers and Finns lived there for several generations. Why did the Topmans have such a brief Island stay? Were they amongst the people repelled by the Island, or did some sudden tragedy or chance of circumstance strike? In some cases a short tenure could have been the result of financial circumstances, such as when Benjamin Salmon sold the Island to Edward Twelawny "for a trifling consideration", after having only purchased the Island from Burthogge Mayow some thirteen years earlier. Burthogge himself clearly had no sentimental attachment to the Island either, as he sold it within a year of purchasing it from his father Philip.

The place of birth is another intriguing aspect of Looe Island residents, for whilst most Island residents were inhabitants of Looe and its surrounding hinterland, records held in Looe Old Guildhall Museum show that the Dix family, who lived on the Island in the early twentieth century, had a five and a half month old baby who was registered as having been born in the USA.

Attie's memoirs notwithstanding, to the best of my knowledge, no other local historian has documented the day to day lives of twentieth century Looe Island residents. By contrast, the amateur historian, Miss Steed Shapcott, kept detailed records about life on Looe Island and the surrounding mainland during the nineteenth century. Although Miss Steed Shapcott oral history accounts were collected in 1928, her interest was not focused on the present, but centred on stories recounted by elderly residents of Looe, who were recalling bygone days; Miss Steed Shapcott's work has proved a useful reference source for writers studying the 'smuggling era' of the eighteenth and nineteenth centuries in particular, and it is largely due to her work that so much is known about some of the Islands more colourful characters. With regard to twentieth century records of Island life, one of the best sources of information are old newspaper articles, and we know from an article in *the Cornish Times,* dated 1929, that a whale, described as a Portugal whale, was washed up on Jetty Beach. There is no such species of whale as a Portugal Whale, and possibly this was a local name for the Fin Whale, which appears to be the most likely candidate from the photographic evidence.

The photograph, accompanying the *Cornish Times article,* and reproduced in Mike Dunn's Book[cxvi] shows six men standing on the back of the whale, all joining hands and three more standing beside it. There is also an enigmatic image on the horizon which could be of a man on horseback.   The whale was subsequently disposed of, by way of being blown up by explosives, and there is an account that one of the men engaged in this operation was showered with stinking whale flesh in the process[cxvii] a small portion of the whale was transported by rail to the British Museum for identification and reportedly the smell on Liskeard Station was so great that the whale part had the a whole carriage to itself. As for the horse and rider, whilst it looks eerily convincing on the photograph, once I enlarged the image on my computer screen, I had to go along with the prosaic conclusion that, the 'horse and rider' are, in reality only the effects of shadows cast on Island House.

As is so often the case, local history will mirror the wider national picture. Following the dissolution of the monasteries in 1556, when church lands, which had come to the Crown were sold to increase the royal coffers, Looe Island, which formed part of the Trelawne Estate, was also sold. John Trelawny, a staunch Protestant, purchased the estate from the Crown in 1600. However, the custodianship of Looe Island is unclear from this time until 1729, when it was recorded that the Island was owned by Philip Mayow. In 1743, Benjamin Salmon, who had only owned it for a relatively brief time (having bought it from Burthogge Mayow in 1730) sold the Island to Edward Trelawny, a relative of John Trelawny. Edward Trelawny was a well-known historical and political figure, being twice MP for West Looe and also Governor of Jamaica. From that time onwards, Looe Island remained in the hands of the Trelawny family, until 1921, when it was sold to

Paul Corder Esq. Although Looe Island was owned by the Trelawny family, who in later years would sometimes use it for hunting and fishing parties, the Island was leased out to different families and inhabited from the eighteenth century onwards by the Finn and Hooper families, who were related to each other and whose smuggling activities have already been recounted. Along with the Trelawny family and the Atkins sisters, Hooper and Finn will remain as names inextricably linked to the history of Looe Island.

Chapter 17

Partings

During my final morning on Looe Island, I stood on the shore with Attie and Val, the sky really was "rosy fingered" and the sea "wine-dark". My Cornish Odyssey was drawing to a close and, although unknown and unconsidered then, I would never see Attie and Babs again; nor would I step onto that sand, jewelled with pebbles and shells, and view the Island with the eyes of a young person embarking on one of life's great adventures.

Eyes fixed on the horizon, watching for the little boat that would take me home, images of the Island's past unfurled in front of me, the dramas, the tragedies the secrets taken to the grave. The two Benedictine monks who had formed their religious cell on the highest point of the Island; The Christ child Jesus, playing on the shores; Elizabeth Hooper grieving for her drowned son; feisty "Black Joan" hoodwinking the gullible customs officials and maybe luring Tom Fletcher away from the law to the world of smuggling. Daffodil growing, shotgun wielding, Major Rawlins, frightening off sightseers; Mr Whitehouse finding the charred remains of his pet monkeys and, of course Attie and Babs, the end of their story as yet unwritten.

Keeping in touch, whilst living a student life, involved letter writing, or finding a working phone box, I seem to remember that Val was the only volunteer that I exchanged addresses with, although Meg and I made many promises to each other about keeping in touch. As I write this, I wonder about those four people, who were such an integral part of my life for a few weeks, before, as ships in the night, we drifted past each other.

Finally, my journey ended at Birmingham's New Street Station. My kind-hearted Mum was there to greet me, and as I alighted from the train, I turned round to have one final look at the Cornishman; but the pixie that I imagined sitting on the front of the engine was not there.

Authors note:- The early steam version of The Cornishman really did have a stylized pixie at the front; but the 1970s train that I travelled on was diesel, and only had the name plate to indicate 'destination Cornwall'.

Looe Island from Hannafore Point (Carolyn Clarke June 2013)

Part 2

Forty Years Later

Chapter 1

Thoughts on past and present

I always knew that one day I would return to my Circean Island, for, like the mythical sirens of old, it would call me back. As I worked through the practicalities of organising my stay in Looe, I recalled the four young volunteers who had worked with me on the Island, all of us on the cusp of planning our future lives and careers. And today, with our life paths largely ordered, we are all probably contemplating our retirements. Time passes, we are all older now than Attie and Babs were then. A decade has passed since Babs died on the Island in 2004, and yet the tenuous chain of continuity exists in the presence of the sisters' friends, Sheila and Gus, who now live on in *Smugglers' Cottage*. In the spirit of the sisters, when I wrote to Sheila she replied with a handwritten letter giving me details of Mrs Hockin's B&B in West Looe where we would be well looked after.

History is about change and continuity; both are present and inextricably linked in the Looe Island story. The age-old Glastonbury Thorn Tree died in 2011, this sacred tree which formed part of the Joseph of Arimathea myth, linking the Island chapel to the See of Glastonbury, met its demise, not through natural causes, but because it was severely vandalized in 2011. The desecration of the thorn tree is no surprise, for holy and sacred places will often attract negative and dark forces. Pilgrims were drowned on their journey to Looe Island, and in its time, the Island has seen violence, murder and theft. It has been overrun by rats and at least one of the former inhabitants was prepared to fire warning shots at those who ventured too close to its shores. Attie herself talked of the Island's power to attract and repel, but now there is no Attie to pass on Looe Island's stories and therefore relatively few visitors would learn that Jesus might have once walked there. Sheila told me in her letter that fewer people visit Looe Island than in the days of the Atkins sisters[cxviii], but in a positive way, this would perhaps enable the Island to 'grow' more in its new role as a conservation and wildlife haven.

These days there are no longer concerns about the Island's future. Thanks to the generosity of the Sister's bequest, the Island was left to Cornwall Wildlife Trust to be managed as a nature reserve, thus, its role as a haven for wildlife has been secured for the foreseeable future and its ecology and biodiversity is more interesting than it could ever have been in those days of the past, when humans deliberately or inadvertently 'interfered' with the landscape, in order to eke out a living. Nonetheless, as the focus of the Island shifts away from the personalities that shaped its past, towards providing a maritime environment for the future, some may say that the Island might never again have such a rich human story to tell.

*

Counting the days to my return to Looe Island, I mulled over how much I have learnt about its colourful past, as I recall and re-live my volunteer days and research the history of the Island. Attie will always remain an enigma to me. During my time on the Island, she told many tales about the people that she knew and who had helped make her dream a reality. As I re-read *Tales from our Cornish Island* I feel I know these characters, some of them, such as Phil and Wren Toms, were people that I really had met and talked to all those years ago, yet Attie's book is prefaced by a disclaimer that *"the characters and situations in this book are entirely imaginary and bear no relation to any real person or actual happening"*[cxix]. I cannot imagine brave Attie fearing libel cases against her, so can only assume that the disclaimer was written tongue in cheek. Perhaps there were exaggerations in her Tales, but imaginary they were not. I knew Attie well enough and heard some of those stories over 40 years earlier.

As I try to conjure up the 'real Attie' she again slips away. I knew some parts of her character well and yet she will always remain an enigma; this highly intelligent, practical person with a phenomenal memory and a gift for making things happen, also believed in strange and mystical powers associated with the Island, she believed in ghosts and buried treasure and willingly accepted the authenticity of a treasure map without making any serious efforts to have it properly dated. Nonetheless, for all the paradoxes surrounding Attie, she was one of life's great givers and the unshakeable passion for the Island that she and Babs shared is their lasting gift to Cornwall.

As outlined earlier, Attie and Babs had very advanced ideas for their time with regard to using only eco-friendly measures and products to eradicate any pests on their crops. Nonetheless, environmental concerns with regards to coastal islands have moved on since the sisters' days. Today, the introduction of livestock requires careful consideration as to what types would be most beneficial in encouraging biodiversity on the Island, and the whole idea of self-sufficiency had been re-thought by the second decade of the twenty first century, with concepts such as sustainable and renewable power sources, which were largely unknown, or certainly not mainstream in the 1970s, when the major part of the Island's lighting and heating was by an oil-fired generator.

Of course, using and living off the Island with some degree of self-sufficiency, has always been the aim of past owners and tenants. The Trelawny's changed the whole Island eco-system with the introduction of a woodland area (largely composed of sycamore trees) to afford some protection from the prevailing south westerly winds and provide cover for game shooting. Later, fields of cultivated daffodils and early potatoes formed part of the Island economy, together with various experiments with everything from goats to bees. Today, the Island still needs to be economically viable and without management the original woodland, planted in Victorian times could encroach on the whole Island.

These days the Island income comes largely from donations and fees from ventures such as Island weddings and holidays. Different types of renewable energy are constantly being sourced to reduce the usage of the fossil fuelled generator and waste is carefully managed though recycling and reuse. As for the sycamore trees, when they die they are replaced by native species, such as oak, ash and predominately hawthorn, whilst the introduction of Hebridean sheep keeps the scrub and grassland in check, so that the coastal grassland, which is suitable for nesting seabirds, can flourish. Elsewhere, areas of grassland are managed for the benefit of wildflowers and invertebrates. In addition, solar panels have been installed on all the Island houses and the generator running times restricted. Logs from the woodland are prepared and used in wood burners.[cxx] The fresh spring water and the collected rainwater is used sparingly, and reused whenever possible and there are also more facilities to collect and store rainwater than there were in the sisters' days. To preserve the fragile environment of the Island, access to key parts are managed to reduce disturbance to wildlife, especially nesting and migratory seabirds, reliant on the Island as a stopping point on their journeys across the continents.

Chapter 2

First sighting

The journey seemed quicker than it had four decades ago, but then, time tends to contract as one grows older. This railway terminus at least was one aspect of Looe that remained unchanged; for Looe station was just as I remembered, with a view of the sea as you entered the town and the line terminating at the end of the platform. Looe is a well-served branch line from Liskeard with about eight trains back and forth every weekday.

Our accommodation was in West Looe and as we crossed the 13 arched bridge from East Looe and the main shopping area of the town I understood why I had failed to spot the Island on my arrival at the railway station all those years ago Looe is divided into East and West Looe, the town is split by the River Looe which flows into the sea at Looe Harbour. On both sides the buildings are largely sited on the hillside of the river valley, but the west side of the valley is steeper than the east, it is also densely wooded in parts and therefore, unsurprisingly, the main concentrations of buildings, including the railway station, are in East Looe. As Looe Island lies on the rocky west side of Looe it is only visible once you cross the bridge to West Looe and start walking away from the town up towards Hannafore Point in the direction of Talland and Polperro.

The old fisherman's café along the harbour side in East Looe was no longer there in the same incarnation, but the buildings looked essentially as I remembered them.

Looe is a very ancient settlement and many of the buildings are timber framed and quaint and crooked. The steepness of the west coastline and the shallow rocky waters between Hannafore and the Island also explain why, despite the Island being so close to the mainland, Looe Island has to be approached by way of the deeper waters of its eastern side.

Having dropped off our bags, I set off to walk along Hannafore Point with my friend Patrick. We had arrived in the middle of the heatwave of June 2013 when temperatures had broken the 1976 records. What a wonderful time to have chosen to return! The sea was azure and turquoise, the sky clear blue and a warm sea breeze was brushing our faces as we climbed up towards Hannafore point. Below the path sea thrift and rock samphire clung to the rocks, punctuated by drifts of moon daisies and vivid clumps of purple and yellow vetches, whilst in flatter parts, areas of grass had been bleached to gold by the unremitting June sun. Below we caught sight of seagulls, cormorants, rock pipits, and oystercatchers and rather bizarrely, a heron was also wading in the shallow water, fishing for sand eels. I intuited that it must have decided to make its way down from the estuary above Looe Harbour, where there are several large heronries and colonies of little egrets, the latter being a relative newcomer to the UK and one which has recently been given 'British Bird 'status due to the success this attractive, dainty, stork-like creature has had in colonizing parts of southern England.

As we walked on, the road continued to rise steeply, then suddenly, as if by magic, we turned a corner and the Island appeared. This walk and the first sighting of the Island, was often described by Attie in her books and now I too was experiencing the view of Looe Island that had captured the sisters' imagination and won their hearts. The Island, rising, indeed almost floating, on the waters like some gigantic turtle, with its 'neck' being formed from a narrow spit of land where *Island House* and *Jetty Cottage* were situated, whilst a wide sandy shore with *Smugglers' Cottage* built on the rocks above it, directly faced us as we looked down from Hannafore Point.

Our walk coincided with low tide, and for the first time since Looe Island had captured my imagination all those years ago, I appreciated how close the Island was to the Hannafore coastline; the waters were very shallow, and festooned with shiny ribbons of yellow and brown kelp and delicate fronds of green and red seaweed. As the light moved on the waters, I caught occasional glimpses of the rocky path that the pilgrims would have used to walk over to the Island chapel and the occasional breaks in the rock where the courageous might have tried to row to its shores. Although the Island is undeniably close to the shore, when we saw these lines of sharp rocks it was self-evident that it would be a brave and foolhardy person who would choose to approach the Island from this direction. Those pilgrims who chose to take their chances and steer their boats between these rocks, rather than wait for the rare low tides that revealed the rocky sea bed path, were often drowned in shipwrecks and even the Smugglers who knew the positions of the rocks intimately, and were skilled at weaving between them and through to the caves at the bottom of the Island, were not always immune from death by shipwreck.

After gazing at the Island for a few minutes and taking some photographs, we found a café overlooking the Island and whilst Patrick (in the best tradition of the tourist) went to buy ice cream cornets, I spoke to a young couple from Plymouth who told me that they spent nearly every weekend here as they just loved Looe so much. They were enthralled when I told them some stories about the Island and there and then they decided to book up a boat trip to Looe Island. Sadly, my conversation with this bright and enthusiastic couple did tend to reinforce Sheila's views that fewer people visited the Island or knew about its history these days. Nonetheless, there is still a steady stream of visitors in good weather, the exact number of boats a day being dependent on the tide, sea state, and demand from tourists.

The system of booking a boat trip involved finding one of the Island's dedicated boats then writing your name on a list kept in a little cabinet alongside the Looe Island Nature Reserve information board on the quayside in East Looe. We signed up for the following day when we would be joined by Patrick's friend Steve, who was in Falmouth at the time, helping to re-paint his friend's boat. Mrs Hockin said that we were lucky to be here whilst the weather was so settled, as a number of trips to the Island had had to be cancelled last year due to inclement weather; once again evidence that Looe Island was logistically near, but often geographically isolated from the mainland.

Chapter 3

The Return

Looe has a reputation that everybody knows everyone else. It is a friendly, close knit community and many of its inhabitants are related to one another. As the sisters had been a part of the Looe community for many years, it came as no surprise that the boatman taking us across to Looe Island remembered them. What was more remarkable was that he also knew of Wren Toms and was able to tell me that he had died a few years ago after having emigrated to America. I wonder where else in England you could mention a person whom you had casually met forty years earlier and the person you spoke to would know them. Clearly the fishing community was a close one, as a couple of days later when taking a boat trip from Polperro to Looe, the boatman on this trip also knew Wren Toms, whom he described as a 'character'. This man added that when he was a schoolboy he had been taught by Babs. I think, from his tales he might have needed a bit of taming in the classroom, for he described Babs as 'very strict'.

On approaching the Island shores the wardens, Claire and Jon were there to greet us, they had brought over a steel jetty, made by Jon, that allowed us to land without wet feet, and a lot more easily than in the days when the Island's volunteers had to catch a rope thrown out from the boat and drag it onto the shore, then push the beached boat back into the waters once the visitors had alighted. Much to Patrick's delight, a sandwich tern had joined the wardens in welcoming us to the Island. The bird had entertained us throughout our journey as it followed the boat over from Looe, seeking fish in the deepening channel between the mainland and the Island shores. Finally as we stepped onto the steel landing trolley, it briefly circled round the boat before proceeding to make its way back to the open sea. Later the sighting of the sandwich tern proved to be of additional interest, as it was found to be one of only two species of birds spotted that day, which had not already been noted in the sisters' own records of Looe Island bird life[cxxi]

Claire then introduced herself and gave us a copy of our self-guided trail. The map showed one trail around the island with an option to cut through the woods. As keen ornithologists, Patrick and Steve's main objective was to watch and record the sea bird life and butterflies, whilst I wanted to take photographs and talk to Claire about the Island's role in the twenty first century, and to also meet Sheila and record the wildflowers that I saw. In retrospect we should have hired the Island's tipi rather than stay on the mainland, as the tides only allow you up to two hours on the Island and there was a lot to do. Still, as Sheila later reminded me, I need not wait another 40 years before coming back. In fact, I knew as soon as I saw the Island again that I would soon want to return.

As we walked up towards the tractor shed my eyes turned towards to a pile of driftwood and rusty metal. Claire said that any interesting flotsam and jetsam that had been washed up onto the shore were kept in this pile. I thought to myself that Attie and Babs would have loved the driftwood and no doubt would have worked it into beautiful objects. The rusty metal pieces were thought to be the debris from a Victorian boat house on the Island, which had been washed away by a big storm shortly after my visit in the 1970s. However, as I looked at the items piled up on the path, I wondered if there could also have been some pieces of a B17 Flying Fortress that had landed in the sea off East Looe during the Second World War, having been damaged by the enemy fire in a bombing raid over Germany[cxxii]. Fortunately the pilot and his crew had managed to parachute to safety. On returning home I found the following Internet posting about the crash; the article serves as yet another example of the historical richness of Looe Island.

> The crew of a Fortress aeroplane B17 Flying Fortress 42-31559 baled out over the land and the aeroplane crashed in Looe Bay, South East Cornwall On the 20th March 1944.
>
> The B17 had been part of the 96th BG at Snetterton Heath in Norfolk and had been on a bombing raid over Germany but, having sustained damage, had lost direction and ended up over Cornwall. A local man tells how the plane came over in a horseshoe pattern from the direction of Morval and how he saw several of the crew parachute out over farmland near Bray.

The plane went on over the sea, out of view and several Looe boys, now in their 70s, have shared their memories of seeing the plane crash into the sea. The pilot, R.G. Dennison was rescued by George Love and Mrs Pearce who rowed out in a leaking boat. Subsequent interest in the accident has mainly centred on the remains of the plane.

People locally, remember the wheels being on the quay shortly after the crash. In the 1970s, some local divers rescued parts of the plane, but could not find anywhere to place them, so they were put back. The engine is being prepared for display in the museum in Looe and it will be accompanied by notes and pictures illustrating the whole story, both of the crash and the subsequent recovery of the artefacts and many details of the story. The 2 propellers have gone to the small aircraft museum at St Mawgan [cxxiii]

*

The Island trail, which provided an option of cutting back through the woodland, started off from the old tractor shed, where jams, made from fruits grown on the Island, and copies of Attie's two published books were for sale.

One wall of the tractor shed was completely lined with secondhand books from Attie and Bab's own bookshelves, which were now being sold to raise money for Cornwall Wildlife Trust. Fittingly their books on wildlife and local history have been kept to form part of the island's heritage, but these eclectic sisters also possessed many novels from the first half of the twentieth century. A quick browse revealed Twentieth Century authors, such as Compton MacKenzie and Graham Greene amongst the remaining books. We all three felt that *Travels with my Aunt*, which I remember Attie saying that she enjoyed reading, might be an appropriate title to purchase, but perhaps predictably, it was no longer on the shelves.

Opposite the tractor shed were tea and coffee making facilities and a picnic bench, the paper cups being 100% biodegradable and used for compost, the results of which could be seen in the shape of a verdant vegetable garden near to Island House. Claire explained that this "Self-service for a donation" scheme, is a trial and depending on its success, the Wardens may, or may not, continue to offer the tea/coffee. In accordance with the philosophy of the Island, the sugar/tea/coffee/longlife milk provided is either organic and/or Fairtrade.

Although I knew that Attie and Babs grew vegetables, which they fertilized with seaweed and kitchen waste, the memory of what they grew and where it was, has eluded me beyond recalling my digging over an area for planting. Nonetheless, Attie's *Tales from our Cornish Island* does describe the fertility of the Island, and the size and quantity and quality of vegetables growing there now proves that point. It was also very heartwarming to know that this Island tradition of self-sufficiency is being continued. In fact Claire had already informed us that Cornwall Wildlife Trust were endeavouring to keep the 'spirit of the sisters' alive on the Island, with the only real changes made being of an environmentally positive nature, such as the replacement of dead sycamore trees from the woodland with native species, whilst the wood was harvested to help with winter heating. The fecundity of the Island vegetable gardens and little wooden plaques of butterfly paintings placed around the Island, so reminiscent of the Speckled Wood plaque on the shelves of Island House circa 1970, began to prove that Cornwall Wildlife Trust were indeed keeping the spirit of the sisters alive.

After walking a few yards along the main shingle path which lead to Island House and one that I remembered so well from my volunteer days, *Smugglers' Cottage* peeped out from the edge of the wooded slopes beyond. The front door was open and Sheila and Gus's two dogs in the garden, their old Bassett Hound had his nose against the wicket gate at the bottom of the path leading up to their front door and wagged his tail in greeting. I hoped that I would be able to talk with Sheila later.

Keeping along the main path we soon came face to face with Mr Whitehouse's carved stone monkeys peering at us through a garland of ivy on the walls of *Island*

House and looking suspiciously like a row of aged tin soldiers scratching their chins. *Island House* itself looked the same as I remembered, apart from the addition of solar panels. It was so good to know that, at least for the time being, *Island House* is home to Mary and Patrick, who have such strong connections to Looe Island.

Island House June 2013. Unchanged from the 1970s apart from the addition of solar panels (Carolyn Clarke June 2013)

Further along the path was *Jetty Cottage*, home to the Wardens. The main room of the cottage also doubled up as a venue for Island weddings, Claire later sent me a photograph to show the room decorated up for wedding receptions; and, as I studied the photograph, I could still see traces of the cream-coloured Island tearoom, set out with its dark wooden tables and filled with light from the low windows looking out onto the garden. Beyond *Jetty Cottage* nestled a dilapidated white shed, which was once the Volunteers Hut. This building, which provided accommodation for volunteers, post- dated my time on Looe Island, but, with its peeling paintwork and rotten timbers, looked at least fifty years old and had become an integral part of the Island landscape. There are no longer any traces of the three wooden huts that we all lived in during our time on the Island. Mary informed me that she remembered two of the huts being in use as volunteer accommodation in 1979 and the third was used as a kitchen hut for volunteers, this is still standing and is used for storage. Whilst one of the two remaining accommodation chalets did eventually rot into the ground, the third has survived and is now in use as a bird hide.

Interior of Jetty Cottage set out for an Island wedding. Courtesy of Cornwall Wildlife Trust

Exterior of Jetty Cottage (Carolyn Clarke June 2013)

*

At the chapel site, Patrick and Steve left me to take photographs whilst they made their way to the bird hide (wherein I might have once slept!), in the hope of spotting interesting sea birds, and perhaps also getting a sighting of the grey seals that inhabit the waters surrounding the Island. The hide is one of the very few additions since my time there, for in those days Attie and Babs would press their eyes to the long-vanished telescope in the hope of identifying some of the interesting sea birds that had settled on the nearby cliffs and rocks.

On looking at the chapel site, I was reminded of how quickly nature heals a landscape. Some five years earlier the site had been extensively dug and documented by Channel Four Time Team, yet to look at it now was to see exactly the same scene of the two lichen-painted marker stones that I had witnessed in the 1970s. Nonetheless, a closer inspection and comparison with earlier photographs revealed that several of the larger stones unearthed by the Time Team, had been left uncovered as further evidence of the chapel's ancient past. Now, thanks to the work of the Time Team I was also aware of the ancient ditch around the site, which I had not noticed in my earlier volunteering days.

A short walk along the western face of the Island and I found the ancient standing stone that looked directly out to the overgrown excavations of the Lamanna chapel complex. We then walked through the woodland, noting that many of the wildflowers recorded by Attie and Babs were still growing in the woodlands and clumps of thrift and stonecrop continued to paint the cliff faces, as they doubtlessly had since the first pilgrims had set foot on the Island.

On the side of the hills Hebridean sheep peacefully grazed, and we watched the butterflies fluttering in the wind, meadow browns, hedge browns, skippers, commas, peacocks, ringlets, speckled woods and large and small whites. Patrick and Claire later discussed the conundrum of the marbled white butterfly, for these beautiful creatures can be found regularly darting amongst the grasses on the coastal footpath that heads west from Hannafore towards Talland. Indeed, when we walked to Polperro the following day we counted over thirty marbled white butterflies along this stretch of the walk. Nonetheless, these butterflies seem strangely reluctant to cross the short stretch of sea between the mainland and the Island and it can only be hoped that following years prove as good for butterflies as the summer of 2013, and that one day they decide to brave the waters across to Looe Island as they search for new territories.

June is not a particularly good time of year to spot sea birds, as it is not the key migration time when there would be a great variety of seabirds on the rocks and shores. Instead, during the summer months, a number of birds tend to leave their Island sanctuary for the open sea. Nonetheless, gulls are still plentiful and Patrick and Steve recorded three different types of gull, there were also cormorants, assiduously drying themselves with outstretched wings on the ragged outcrop of rocks beyond the Island as swallows flew above, and there were oystercatchers, turnstones, rock pipits and a grey wagtail.

Interestingly, the grey wagtail is not recorded on the Atkins sisters' list and, although their sightings were not scientific or definitive, they were knowledgeable ornithologists and the distinctive little grey wagtail with its slate-grey back and bright yellow breast was not a bird that they would have overlooked. This does tend to indicate that it could be a relatively new visitor to the Island, as the sisters' list was compiled over many days and a number of years and certainly included the grey wagtail's more common cousin, the pied wagtail.

Today, under the auspices of Cornwall Wildlife Trust records of the species of birds sighted are kept by the Wardens, and every month volunteers/experts who record for the Trust and are linked to Looe Marine Conservation Group and Cornwall Seal Group, also visit the Island to record its birds and monitor the nesting seabirds. There is also a ringing project for the Great black-backed gulls. The latter two projects involve members of Cornwall Bird Watching and Preservation Society.

Since my volunteer days, I have had lasting memories of the bats that flew round the Island on warm summer nights. One of the questions I wanted to ask Claire was concerning whether the Island still had a bat colony or two; much to my delight, she informed me that since she and Jon had moved to the Island in 2004, Common Pipistrelle, Daubenton's and Lesser Horseshoe bat have all been recorded. Claire then explained that the bats could be seen (and heard with the aid of a bat detector) all over the island and especially around the 'meadows' and woodland edge/hedges, and the sheltered coastline on the eastern side of the island. The bats are encouraged to continue making the Island their home by bat boxes being placed on some of the trees and the Island gardens being managed to encourage the night-flying insects which they feed on. My mind went back to Attie and Babs and their love of the natural world and how pleased they would be to discover that the ecological health of the Island was strong and that the number of different species there was steadily increasing[cxxiv].

One Island visitor that we had all hoped to see was the grey seal[cxxv]. Patrick thought that their absence was due to the heat wave, which would have caused them to swim out to the cooler waters of the open sea; one particular famous seal of Looe Island was Nelson, who is immortalized in a life-size bronze statue on the West Quay. This veritable old man of the sea, (called Nelson because he only had one eye) chose the rocks of Looe Island as his home, but today at least, we were not blessed with the site of any of his progeny basking in the Island waters.

The men then went to get a cup of coffee whilst I returned to the tractor shed with Claire, she told me a little bit about changes in the management of the Island since the sisters' time and promised to send me details of ventures such as weddings. Claire suggested that I tried calling from the wicket gate at *Smugglers' Cottage* to see if Sheila was about.

A few minutes later I was sitting on a bench outside *Smugglers' Cottage* with Sheila whilst we reminisced about Island life in the 1970s and the Atkins sisters. Sheila told me of her sadness in watching the strong, independent Babs being gradually weakened by the leukemia which eventually took her life. Sheila also talked of earlier times and told of her own personal involvement in the divining exercise to try and locate the Island 'treasure' which turned out to be a large stone found under the lawn of Island house. When talking of days past, Sheila also recalled how sometimes she and Gus missed the active involvement that they used to have in Island life with Gus taking guided tours round the Island. However, she equally appreciated that now they are both quite elderly, this would no longer be feasible on a regular basis. Conscious that the boat would soon be arriving to pick us up again, I said my goodbyes with promises to keep in touch and not wait another 40 years before returning.

Smugglers Cottage (Carolyn Clarke June 2013)

Chapter 4

Leaving Looe

The Island visit was the main purpose and highlight of my brief Cornish holiday, but there were many other interesting 'Island related' things to do in my remaining couple of days. The following morning I visited the Old Guildhall Museum in East Looe. Here many historical records relating to the Island are stored and the two volunteer guides there gave me a folder full of newspaper clippings and articles from *The Cornish Times to* look through. After reading some of the fascinating accounts of Croft Andrew's excavations we talked about which aspects of Looe Island's history they personally found the most fascinating, for the one Guide it was the story of the beached 'Portugal' Whale which covered one of the men with stinking whale flesh when it was detonated to facilitate its removal from the Island. However, John was most fascinated by the census returns for the Island which showed that John Dix's place of birth was the USA, albeit that he was only 5 and a half months when he was brought by his parents to Looe Island. As would be expected, most Island residents were Cornish people.

Other holiday excursions included a walk to the estuary to see the place where the herons and little egrets had made their home in the wooded areas flanking the estuarine water; then finally a walk to Polperro where we could see for ourselves the clouds of marbled white butterflies that were reluctant to venture across to Looe Island. We walked to Polperro by way of the coastal path and as we stopped for lunch in Talland, I was reminded that it was at Talland Church that the names of the "Chaplains of Lamana on Looe Island" are inscribed, and from where Attie acquired her church organ, and where Hamram and Jochabed Hooper had been christened; sponsored by their well-connected godparents.

Our return to Looe from Polperro was by boat, and once again, the Island suddenly appeared to float onto the horizon. We were so close that I could see all the features and details; the caves, the woods, the dark, fluffy outlines of the Hebridean sheep grazing on the hillside, and the three houses with all the human life, history and secrets they held.

Postscript

The spirit of the Island remains the same, but, as the Twenty first century progresses initiatives have taken place to ensure the Island's sustainability in ecological and financial terms.

Today, visitors can once again stay on Looe Island by hiring the Island's Tipi, and weddings also provide some additional income. Claire explained that when Mary and Patrick were married on the Island, as the chapel had not been consecrated for some time, they arranged for *Jetty Cottage* to be licensed for weddings and bought a wedding licence for the Island; Cornwall Wildlife Trust have since renewed this licence and continue to offer civil wedding ceremonies. Currently a number of Island weddings take place each year and on such occasions part of *Jetty Cottage* is set up for the couple's wedding ceremony. After the ceremony some couples have simple buffet food on the lawn, under a simple marquee set up there, before the wedding party returns to the mainland to continue with their celebrations.

Other initiatives associated with the Island include guided tours by the warden and wildlife news, available on the Island website. The island is within a Voluntary Marine Nature Reserve and is regularly surveyed. The island is currently on a shortlist to be a Marine Conservation Zone as the waters surrounding it which contain some rare and unusual sea life.

All proceeds of this book will go to help the work of Cornwall Wildlife Trust has over 15,000 members who are protecting Cornwall's wildlife and wild places www.cornwallwildlifetrust.org.uk/join.

Contacts

Looe Island Nature Reserve
Cornwall Wildlife Trust
Tel:0797 429 3495
Email:looeisland@cornwallwildlifetrust.org.uk
Website: www.cornwallwildlifetrust.org.uk/looeisland
Facebook: www.facebook.com/CornwallWildlifeTrust

Address: Cornwall Wildlife Trust, Five Acres, Allet, Truro, Cornwall, TR4 9DJ (Registered office)

The Old Guildhall Museum and Gaol
High Market Street,
East Looe
Cornwall

[i] Annotated version of the detailed chronology supplied by Mike Dunn *The Looe Island Story:* Mike Dunn Pub. Polperro Heritage Press 2005 P. 81-84

[ii] Ordnance Survey told Cornwall Wildlife Trust that Looe Island the only place to have two official English names – other places may have two names but they would be translations from languages such as Gaellic

[iii] Island Life – *A History of Looe Island* David David Clensy Pub lulu 2004 P.3

[iv] David Clensy Pub Lulu 2004 ibid

[v] *The Book of Looe* p.24 Camp and Birchwood-Harper Pub. Halsgrove 2007

[vi] The Islanders :From the Barren Mewstone to Looe Island, the Smuggler's Cornish Haven. Pub lulu 2011. Currently this book is out of print

[vii] Email conversation with Barbara Birchwood-Harper May 2013

[viii] September 2012

[ix] Conversation with Sheila Ravine June 2013

[x] *Tales from our Cornish Island* Evelyn E Atkins Pub 1986 Coronet Books (2nd edition) 1987 and *We Bought an Island:* Evelyn E Atkins Pub 1976 George G Harap and Co Ltd

[xi] *Looe Island Story* Mike Dunn Pub. Polperro Heritage Press 2005

[xii] L. P Hartley *The Go-between* Pub Hamish Hamilton 1953

[xiii] www.**looe**.org/**island**.html

[xiv] *Tales from our Cornish Island* Evelyn E Atkins Pub 1986 Coronet Books (2nd edition) 1987 *We Bought an Island* Evelyn E Atkins Pub 1976 George G Harap and Co Ltd

[xv] *Tales from our Cornish Island* Evelyn E Atkins Pub 1986 Coronet Books (2nd edition) 1987

[xvi] P118 *ibid*

[xvii] We Bought an Island Evelyn E Atkins Pub 1976 George G Harap and Co Ltd

[xviii] P. 42 Ibid

[xix] David Clensy Pub Lulu 2004 p 1-6

[xx] Today postcards showing Looe Island were not available for sale in Looe and an Internet search did not show any post-1970s postcards for sale. This reinforces the view tht there is less interest in the Island today than in the time of the Atkins sisters

[xxi] *Tales from our Cornish Island* Evelyn E Atkins Pub 1986 Coronet Books (2nd edition) 1987

[xxii] Island Life – *A History of Looe Island* David David Clensy Pub lulu 2004
[xxiii] Op Cit. We Bought an Island Atkins
[xxiv] Hamram is correctly named Amram but Attie admitted in her book that Hamram was easier to say: Black Joan was the nickname of Jochabed, Amram's sister, but the same name is also attributed to Joan Fynn, wife of John 'Mewstone man'
[xxv] P. 152 Op cit. *Tales* Atkins
[xxvi] Ibid p p155
[xxvii] This would, even these days be an impossible engineering feat
[xxviii] Op Cit. *Tales* Atkins
[xxix] Ibid p155
[xxx] It is only following the Time Team investigations 2008 when the concept of the physical interlinking underground tunnels were proved to be a physical impossibility, that this theory was finally discredited
[xxxi] Ibid
[xxxii] Details of name changes can be found in *The Looe Island Story*. Op Cit P.26
[xxxiii] C4 Time Team 2008
[xxxiv] ibid p.155
[xxxv] Ibid p157-8
[xxxvi] Op cit. *The Book of Looe* p.24 Camp and Birchwood-Harper p.24
[xxxvii] Ibid P.5
[xxxviii] Weatherhill, Craig, Place Names in Cornwall and Scilly, Wessex Books, 2005
[xxxix] *The Looe Island Story:* Mike Dunn p.26
[xl] *Time Team* Channel Four 2008
[xli] Email from Mike Dunn 5 October 2013
[xlii] Op Cit. David Clensy P13-14
[xliii] Op Cit. We Bought an Island Atkins
[xliv] en.wikipedia.org/wiki/Looe_Island
[xlv] Ibid 157-160
[xlvi] Ibid 51-53
[xlvii] Ibid P.48
[xlviii] Op Cit David Clensy P.36
[xlix] *The Looe Island Story:* Mike Dunn Polperro Press P.34
[l] As noted by David Clensy, Rawlins is the correct spelling of the name although he appears as Rawlings in *Tales*
[li] Op Cit. We Bought an Island Atkins p.44
[lii] Ibid P.54
[liii] This fact was verified by a friend of my sister, who lived in Cornwall in the 1980s
[liv] Op Cit. *Tales* 54-63
[lv] Op Cit. David Clensy P88 interview with Babs Atkins Summer 1999
[lvi] This slightly disagrees with the 15 recorded and named by Attie in *Tales*
[lvii] Op Cit. *We Bought an Island* P44-45
[lviii] Ibid P.45

[lix] Email conversation with the Wardens, August 2013
[lx] Op Cit. *Tales* P122-128
[lxi] en.wikipedia.org/wiki/Ictis
[lxii] Now renamed Trelawny Island. in honour of the family who owned Looe Island for so many years. Trelawny Island is, once again, in the ownership of the family, having been bequeathed separately to the family when Babs died in 2004
[lxiii] www.wildlifeextra.com
[lxiv] Rambles Beyond Railways, by Wilkie Collins Pub 1851 *ebooks.adelaide.edu.au/c/collins/wilkie/rambles.../chapter2.html*
[lxv] Ibid
[lxvi] Op Cit. Mike Dunn P.36
[lxvii] Ibid p91-2
[lxviii] Byrne, Paula The Real Jane Austen P.239 Harper Press 2013
[lxix] Clink Prison, Museum Guide. Southwark August 2013
[lxx] Dunn Op cit P.33
[lxxi] On returning to the Island in 2013, the Wardens confirmed that there are no longer any rabbits on the Island
[lxxii] Email correspondence between myself and David Clensy January 2013
[lxxiii] The Observers' Book of Sea and Seashore
[lxxiv] Walking Through History C.4 14 December 2013.
[lxxv] The Smugglers' Banker: The Story of Zephaniah Job of Polperro: Jeremy Rowlett Johns. Cited in an interview Walking Through History C.4 14 December 2013.
[lxxvi] Walking Through History C.4 14 December 2013. **Interview with** Mark Camp, co-author of *The Book of Looe Op cit*
[lxxvii] www.darklingroom.co.uk/thl2/*Smugglers'*_cave.html
[lxxviii] Ibid
[lxxix] Time Team C.4 2008
[lxxx] A farmhouse, no longer standing on the Island
[lxxxi] *A Nest of Smugglers'*Op Cit.
[lxxxii] Email from Barbara Birchwood-Harper 2 February 2012
[lxxxiii] *A Nest of Smugglers'*Op Cit.
[lxxxiv] Ibid.
[lxxxv] Op Cit. Mike Dunn P.82
[lxxxvi] David Clensy Op Cit. P.39
[lxxxvii] Ibid
[lxxxviii] www.theoldbridgehousehotel.co.uk/looe/looe-island/caves
[lxxxix] ibid
[xc] Barbara Birchwood-Harper commented in an email sent 9 February 2012 that she used the name of Anthony Justy Hooper from Morval, in her researches, but cautions that it may well be that another Hooper lies hidden in the indecipherable parish records of another place. It is likely that Anthony is buried on Looe Island. The Finns including John Finn and his wife,

Elizabeth, both sons plus Elizabeth Hooper and her granddaughter are all buried in Morval churchyard.

[xci] Mike Dunn Op Cit. p.65
[xcii] Op Cit. P.24 *The Book of Looe*
[xciii] Email 31 January 2013 Barbara Birchwood-Harper
[xciv] David Clensy Op Cit.
[xcv] Ibid P.37
[xcvi] www.yor-tec.co.uk/cornwall/looe.htm
[xcvii] David Clensy Ibid P.49
[xcviii] Walking Through History C.4 14 December 2013.
[xcix] Barbara Birchwood-Harper – A Nest of *Smugglers*
[c] ibid
[ci] Mike Dunn Op cit. P.66
[cii] ibid
[ciii] ibid Op cit. P.85
[civ] Ibid p.85
[cv] The family's' name also appears is spelt variously as Vague or Veague, which is how it appeared in the local newspaper report recording the birth of Ann
[cvi] Ibid p.85
[cvii] Most recently by both David Clensy and Mike Dunn
[cviii] Reproduced in *The Looe Island Story:* Mike Dunn Op cit P.46
[cix] Email conversation with the Wardens August 2013
[cx] Dunn Op Cit P.48
[cxi] Retrospective views of the sisters gathered through talking to residents of Looe during my return visit June 2013
[cxii] Op Cit.. David Clensy p.93 transcript of an interview with Babs Atkins summer 1999
[cxiii] Ibid P.74
[cxiv] www.monkeysanctuary.org
[cxv] Ibid P.72
[cxvi] Op Cit. *The Looe Island Story:* Mike Dunn P.53
[cxvii] Report in the Cornish Times December 1929 held at Looe Museum
[cxviii] Letter from Sheila Ravine 16 January 2013
[cxix] Evelyn Atkins *Tales from our Cornish Island* Title Page Pub. Coronet 1987
[cxx] Information supplied by email from assistant warden Claire
[cxxi] *Looe Island Story* Mike Dunn Pub. Polperro Heritage Press 2005 P.73
[cxxii] Claire informed me that no pieces of the B17 had been positively identified as having been washed up on the Island. Nonetheless, the proximity of Looe Island to the crash added a tantalising possibility
[cxxiii] WW2 Aircraft Wrecks in the English channel(2008) - Page 2 - Key ...
[cxxiv] As far as I am aware, only Pipistrelle bats were present on the Island in the 1970s, although as the sisters did not keep records of the bat population I cannot be sure of this fact

[cxxv] Claire informed me that grey seals are spotted all year around (in varying numbers) and in all weathers and that they are learning more about them though the Looe Island Seal Photo Identification Project. There are now over 45 grey seals and 2 common seals on our photo identification database. The information is collected from monthly surveys using volunteers from Looe Marine Conservation Group and Cornwall Seal group as well as information collected by us wardens and public sightings of seals

Printed in Great Britain
by Amazon.co.uk, Ltd.,
Marston Gate.